PROFILES OF THE PATRIARCHS

VOLUME TWO

JACOB

HOW AN UNPRINCIPLED PERSON BECAME

A PRINCE WITH GOD

BOOKS BY CYRIL J. BARBER

Successful Church Libraries, with E. Towns
The Minister's Library, 2 vols.
The Minister's Library, vol. 3, with M. L. Bickley
God Has the Answer
Searching for Identity
Nehemiah and the Dynamics of Effective Leadership
Always a Winner, with J. Carter
Vital Encounter
Marriage Enrichment in the Church
Leadership: The Dynamics of Success, with G. Strauss
Introduction to Theological Research
Your Marriage Has Real Possibilities
Ruth: A Story of God's Grace
You Can Have a Happy Marriage
Habakkuk and Zephaniah
Through the Valley of Tears
Your Marriage Can Last a Lifetime
Judges: A Narrative of God's Power
The Books of Samuel, 2 vols.
Best Books for your Home ... Library
Introduction to Theological Research, rev. ed., with R. Krauss, Jr.
Unlocking the Scriptures
Faithfulness of God, 2 vols.
The Books of Kings, 4 vols. in 2.
The Dynamics of Effective Leadership
The Books of Chronicles, 2 vols.
Lord, Please Help Me, My Teenager Is Driving Me Crazy, with G. Strauss.
Joshua: We Will Serve the Lord
Ezra and Esther
Patriarchal Profiles: Abraham and Isaac.
Patriarchal Profiles: Jacob
Contributor, *Zondervan Pictorial Encyclopedia of the Bible*
Contributor, *New Unger's Bible Dictionary*
Contributor, *Baker's Encyclopedia of the Bible*

PROFILES OF THE PATRIARCHS

VOLUME TWO

JACOB

HOW AN UNPRINCIPLED PERSON BECAME A PRINCE WITH GOD

by

CYRIL J. BARBER

WIPF & STOCK · Eugene Oregon

Wipf and Stock Publishers
199 W 8th Ave, Suite 3
Eugene, OR 97401

Profiles of the Patriarchs, Volume 2
Jacob: How an Unprincipled Person Became a Prince with God
By Barber, Cyril J.
Copyright©2010 by Barber, Cyril J.
ISBN 13: 978-1-60899-846-3
Publication date 7/8/2010

Quotations of Scripture used in this book are from the
New American Standard Bible (NASB)
copyrighted 1960, 1962, 1963, 1971, 1973, 1975,
1977, 1995
by the Lockman Foundation, and are
used by permission of the Lockman Foundation.

Other quotations and/or paraphrases of Scripture
are the author's.

Biblical references in parentheses (e.g., 12:1)
are to the book of Genesis.

THIS BOOK IS DEDICATED TO THOSE

SUNDAY SCHOOL TEACHERS,

CHRISTIAN BUSINESS PEOPLE

AND PASTORS

WHO, OVER THE YEARS, CONTRIBUTED

IMMEASURABLY TO MY

SPIRITUAL GROWTH

THE AUTHOR

Cyril J. Barber, D.Litt., D.Min., D.D. is pastor emeritus of Plymouth Church, Whittier, California. He makes his home in Hacienda Heights with Aldyth, his wife of fifty years.

CONTENTS

PREFACE

JACOB

1.	MIDNIGHT FLIGHT	1
2.	TWO IS ONE TOO MANYS	11
3.	POETIC JUSTICE	21
4.	THE LONG ROAD HOME	29
5.	CONFRONTING AN OLD FEAR	39
6.	ONE STEP FORWARD, THREE STEPS BACKL	47
7.	AN EXPENSIVE PRICETAG	55
8.	THE ALL-SUFFICIENT ONE	65
9.	RENEWAL OF THE PROMISE	73
10.	ON THE ROAD AGAIN	79
11.	LOVE'S INDISCRETIONS	89
12.	FAMINE RELIEF	101

PREFACE

It was a common trait among earlier writers to portray Bible characters as flawless saints. To do this they depicted them without defect, and any imperfection was attributed to the society of which they were a part.

In writing about the patriarchs, and in particulare Jacob, I have done so believing that what was written about them is for our instruction (cf. Romans 15:4). By honestly examining Jacob's life, and assessing as best I can his failures, I have endeavored to show God's patience in dealing with him, and how He eventually transformed him into a "prince with God." This study also has impressed upon me the fact that there is a little of Jacob in all of us. We have our moments of spiritual growth that are often followed by lengthy periods of spiritual barrenness.

From what we learn through this process of honestly interacting with the biblical text we come to realize that God's choice of us is based upon His desire to conform us to the image of His Son. It is of great comfort, therefore, to find in the story of Jacob the unvarnished record of a person of like passions with ourselves who became a trophy of His grace.

Sir William Smith, in his *Bible Dictionary*, shares with us his insights into Jacob's character; he appears to have inherited the gentle, quiet, and retiring character of his father along with the self-centered yet prudent cunning from his mother. These traits showed themselves in his reprehensible deception of his father, the means he employed to make his bargain with his uncle (Laban) work to his own enrichment, and his guile in dealing with Esau when invited to visit him at Petra.

In spite of the fact that Jacob came face to face with a heavenly "Visitor" on the banks of the Jabbok, the change wrought did not last for long. It required the increasing revelations of God to enlighten his old age. In the end the man of subtle devices died, and is forever remembered in the covenant formula made with Abraham, Isaac *and* Jacob.

In preparing this book for publication I have refrained from citing biblical references to the book of Genesis in their entirety. Instead, I have cited only by chapter and verse within parrntheses (e.g., 42:1). References to other books of the Bible are cited in full (e.g., Psalm 55:22).

What follows is not for the academic, but a simple work for lay people. To this end it is my constant prayer that what is contained in these pages will be of benefit to them.

I cannot close this introduction without mentioning two men whose respective skills have contributed to this work. They are Maurice Bickley and David Cahn. To them I owe a very profound "Thank you!"

CHAPTER 1

MIDNIGHT FLIGHT

A solitary figure moved silently from shadow to shadow, avoiding the silvery light of the moon that shone down from a cloudless sky.[1] The lone individual who was stealing away from the camp was none other than Jacob, Isaac and Rebekah's younger son. But how can we explain his furtive departure?

Jacob had stolen his twin brother Esau's birthright,[2] and Esau, ever a strong-willed and impetuous person, had vowed to kill him (27:30-36, 41-42). To save Jacob from such a fate Rebekah determined to send him to her brother who lived in Haran, with the avowed purpose of taking a wife from among her relatives[3]. Her real intent was to remove Jacob from the encampment until Esau's wrath

---

1. The air is so clear in these Near Eastern climes that one can walk about at night without stumbling.
2. For the benefits of the birthright, see M. F. Unger, "Inheritance (Hebrew)," in the *New Unger's Bible Dictionary*, revised ed. (Chicago: Moody, 1988), 617-18.
3. In his masterful book *Paradise to Prison* (Grand Rapids: Baker, 1975), 236, John J. Davis has written: "Isaac's dependence upon his five senses resulted in his deception, and this provides a rather subtle warning to all who would depend solely on empirical evidence for truth! Satan has for millennia provided impressive substitutes for the real thing, and unfortunately many do not discover the deception until tragedy has occurred" (27:1-46).

cooled. Then she planned to send for him and bring him home.

Esau possibly learned of this scheme from one of the servants who had overheard Isaac's parting words to Jacob, and he determined to waylay his brother on his way north and kill him. This is why it was necessary for Jacob to secretly leave the tents of his parents at night. He could then put some distance between himself and his brother without Esau knowing which route he had taken.

Jacob's route to Haran was not the same as the one taken by Eliezer when he went north to choose a bride for his father Isaac (24:10-11, 16). He could not afford to pass through or near any city for fear that someone might recognize him. News spread very quickly in these parts and it was important that he leave no trace of his hegira lest Esau track him down. Jacob, therefore, planned to head in a north-easterly direction and cross the River Jordan at a fordable place north of the Dead Sea (note 32:10). Once across the Jordan he would be in an area where His father was unknown, and he could travel with greater freedom. Also, the rugged terrain of the Transjordanian landscape would make it easy for him to hide if Esau should follow him.

As Jacob made his way along the road that led past Hebron he became conscious that this was the first time he had been away from home. He was now facing the unknown. His heart was beating rapidly for fear that someone returning home late at night might see him and tell of it in the local market place. If this happened, it would not take long for Esau to hear of it. And he was also feeling the first pangs of loneliness.

As day dawned he neared Ephrathah (later named Bethlehem). Some farmers were probably stirring, and Jacob hurried past their little village hoping that no one would recognize him. He walked on. Weary mile was being replaced by weary mile. He also paused every now and then to look behind him to see if he was being followed. Even when the sun was at its zenith he continued to put as many miles as possible between himself and Esau.

The day wore on, and as the sun began to decline in the west he reached a place near the city of Luz where rocky pillars reached for the sky. He had covered fifty miles since leaving his home on the plain of Beersheba and now, exhausted from his flight, he selected a flat rock for a pillow and lay down to sleep.[4]

While he slept he dreamed that he saw a stairway[5] stretching from earth to heaven with God's messengers (i.e., angels) ascending and descending on it (28:12). But most

---

4. See William M. Thomson's indispensable *The Land and the Book*, 3 vols. (New York: Harper & Brothers, 1886), I:54. Edward Robinson, *Biblical Researches in Palestine*, 3 vols. (London: Murray, 1856), I:448-50, 575, provides convincing evidence for *Beitin* being the location of Bethel.
5. The KJV translated the Hebrew word "ladder." This was misleading, and most modern translations have followed the precedent set by these early 1611 translators. It is preferable to see here a stairway with the angels of God ascending and descending upon it.

significant of all, the Lord was standing at the head of the stairs.

The stairway symbolized the genuine and uninterrupted fellowship between God in heaven and His people on earth, and the angelic messengers represented the means whereby God constantly took care of His own.

Then the Lord spoke directly to Jacob:

"I am the Lord the God of your father Abraham and the God of Isaac; the land on which you lie, I will give it to you and to your descendants. Your descendants will also be like the dust of the earth, and you will spread out to the west and to the east and to the north and to the south; and in you and in your descendants shall all the families of the earth be blessed. Behold, I am with you and will keep you wherever you go, and will bring you back to this land; for I will not leave you until I have done what I have promised you" (28:13-15).

This was a startling revelation, and we are not surprised that Jacob woke up. God's promises formed a unilateral extension of the Abrahamic covenant (note the repeated use of "I will ..."). The first promise pertained to the land (28:13), and included making his descendants so numerous that they would appear like the dust of the earth, spreading to all points of the compass; the second was the promise of protection (28:15) and graciously granted Jacob assurance of God's presence wherever he might go; and the third was, "I will not leave you ..."--a promise to help Jacob remember that all he did was done with God's eye upon him.

Jacob's response to his dream shows his growing reverence for the Lord. "Surely the Lord is in this place, and I did not know it." Then he felt fear, and said, "How awesome is this place! This is none other than the house of God, and this is the gate of heaven!" (28:16-17).

As the rays of the rising sun began to dispel the darkness Jacob arose and took the stone that had been his pillow, set it upright, and anointed it with some oil from a flask he had with him. He then changed the name of the place from Luz to Bethel (*Beth*, "house," *El* [of] "God"). His vow that followed has caused English readers problems, and many commentators obliquely sidestep the difficulty by declining to make any comment on it. Jacob's vow seems to imply doubt in the Lord's fulfilment of His promises unless he, Jacob, did something to compel God to keep His word. We read:

> "Then Jacob made a vow, saying, 'If God will be with me and will keep me on this journey that I take, and will give me food to eat and garments to wear, and I return to my father's house in safety, then the Lord will be my God. This stone, which I have set up as a pillar, will be God's house, and of all that You give me I will surely give a tenth to You'" (28:20-22).

Learned Semitic scholars tell us that, though Jacob's vow sounds like he was placing conditions on God's unilateral covenant, this was in reality a Hebrew way of accepting what the Lord had said.

And with that the chapters ends.

It now remains for us to draw principles from what the Holy Spirit has revealed to us. If possible discuss the following with a friend.

- As we read between the lines of 28:1-4 we note that a reconciliation had taken place. Isaac was not the kind of person to compromise, and so there must have been confession on the part of Rebekah and Jacob, and Isaac's forgiveness of them. Initially this seems strange, seeing forgiveness is not mentioned in the passage before us. On closer examination, however, we note Isaac's wholehearted blessing of Jacob. For these sentiments to be sincere there must have been a restoration of their relationship. (Isaac was wise enough to realize that Jacob could not have acted alone, for how could he have covered his arms and neck with goat's hair without someone's help. His helper must have been his mother.)

   Both Rebekah and Isaac must have confessed their sin, and Rebekah may have excused her actions by telling her husband what the Lord had told her many years earlier, namely, that "the elder son would serve the younger one" (25:23). Isaac would then have realized how grievous a mistake he would have made had he given the birthright to Esau. This does not excuse Rebekah's deceit, and perhaps at last she began to realize how wrong she had been to withhold information from him.

   And so, with Isaac's blessing, Jacob was sent to Haran to obtain a wife from his mother's people.

- Second, Jacob's vision at Bethel impressed upon him the ministry of angelic beings. (The Hebrew *mal`ak* and the Greek *angelos*, both mean "messenger"). Angels are personal, sinless, immortal beings, existing in great number, and in close relation not only with individuals but also vitally involved in the work of God's Kingdom.

  We are dependant wholly upon the Scriptures for our knowledge of angelic beings. Biblical revelation teaches us that they are involved in worship and set before us an example of joyous and perfect fulfillment of God's will (e.g., in the words, "Thy will be done in earth *as it is in heaven* [i.e., by angels, see Matthew 6:10], and "There is joy in the presence of the angels of God over one sinner who repents" (Luke 15:10)). Furthermore, their ministry reminds us of the goodness of God who sends His angels "to render service for the sake of those who will inherit salvation" (Hebrews 1:14; cf. 12:22).

- Third, the covenant the Lord made with Jacob indicates (among other things) his election to a position of privilege. In 25:23 we are told that before the twins were born and neither of them had done anything good or bad. So that God's purpose according to His choice would stand it was told Rebekah, "The older will serve the younger" (cf. Romans 9:10-13).

  In extending His covenant to include Jacob the Lord was bestowing a great honor upon him by including him with Abraham and Isaac, through whose descendants blessing would come upon all the nations on the earth. Jacob was overawed by the promise the Lord had made him, but it took time and personal growth before he began to live up to the privilege bestowed upon him.

As far as we are concerned, God's mercy is unearned (John 17:2, 9; Romans 8:29). Those who have accepted Christ live within the sphere of God's special grace. The privileges they enjoy are not based upon their works (Ephesians 2:8-9), wisdom, nobility, or wealth (1 Corinthians 1:26-29), but solely upon God's love. Their response is to grow in grace and in a knowledge of all that Christ has done for them (Colossians 2:6-7, 3:12-13; 1 Peter 2:9; 2 Peter 1:10-11).[6]

There are some who resist the Gospel message by claiming that they are not numbered among the elect. But how do they know this? I have never seen a list containing the names of those whom God has sovereignly called to be saved. During His earthly ministry the Lord Jesus said of some who heard Him preach, "you are unwilling to come to Me so that *you may have life*" (John 5:40), and again, "Come to Me, *all* who are weary and heavy-laden, and *I will give you rest*. Take My yoke upon you and learn from Me, for I am gentle and humble in heart, and you will find rest for your souls. For My yoke is easy and My burden is light" (Matthew 11:28-30, emphasis added. See also Ephesians 1:4-7).

---

6. Henry Holloman provides an important discussion of this topic in his *Kregel Dictionary of the Bible* (Grand Rapids: Kregel, 2005), 127-28.

By including Jacob in the covenant God had made with Abraham, He conferred on him a great honor, for the carrying out of God's promise would result in bringing blessing to people all over the world.

CHAPTER 2

TWO IS ONE TOO MANY

Hebrew is a fascinating language. We read that Jacob, encouraged by God's revelation to him, "picked up his feet" and continued his long journey to the steppes of Aram (Syria) at the west end of the Euphrates River. When he reached his destination he had traversed more than five hundred miles. Foot-sore, homesick, and with feelings of mingled anxiety and anticipation, he arrived penniless in the "land of the sons of the east."

The Meeting at the Well (29:1-14). Jacob had seen the whitewashed walls of a city in the distance, and made his way toward it. On the outskirts he came across a well with three flocks of sheep lying lazily on the ground while the shepherds stood idly by occupying whatever shade was available to them. Being cautious, Jacob began by asking questions:

"My brothers, where are you from?"

They responded by saying, "We are from Haran."

At this Jacob's heart skipped a beat. He had come to the right place. He then asked, "Do you know Laban the son of Nahor?"

To this question they said somewhat guardedly, "We know him."

Jacob then asked, "Is it well with him?"

They responded, "It is well, and here is Rachel his daughter coming with the sheep."

On hearing this, Jacob wanted to be alone with Rachel and so suggested that because there were still many hours before nightfall, the shepherds water their sheep and then take them out to pasture.

Their reply indicated their inertia: "We cannot water our flocks until all the flocks are gathered. Then they roll the stone from the mouth of the well. Only then can we water the sheep" (29:4-8).

While Jacob was still speaking with them, Rachel came with her father's sheep. According to 29:17*b* she was "beautiful of form and face," and Jacob was instantly attracted to her. She was the first member of his extended family that he had seen, and forgetting how tired he was and how far he had come, and wanting to impress her with his physical prowess, he took a firm hold of the stone that covered the mouth of the well and moved it without anyone's help. Jacob was then free to water Laban's sheep, and once this was done he kissed Rachel passionately. With the doubt and uncertainty of the past several weeks removed, the floodgates of Jacob's pent-up feelings were opened, and he gave way to a torrent of tears.

Rachel, of course, was overcome with awe. Who was this stranger?

When Jacob had sufficiently recovered, he told Rachel that he was her father's nephew and her aunt Rebekah's son (29:12), and she ran and told her father of his arrival. Jacob, of course, received a hearty welcome. But where were the camels laden with gifts? Years earlier when Eliezer had been sent to select a wife for Isaac he had arrived with servants and supplies, costly jewelry and gorgeous attire. By contrast, Jacob came to Laban's home with only a sturdy staff. Dr. William H. Thomson, son of the famous author of *The Land and the Book*, and for many years a medical doctor in Palestine and Syria, wrote:

> "Had Jacob not cheated his father and thus incurred the deadly enmity of Esau, he could very well have obtained from his parents such an outfit for his journey to Padan-Aram as became the son of an Emir richer now than Abraham was, in the quest for such a wife as Isaac and Rebekah would approve of. His camels would have been laden with all kinds of presents, and with silver and gold which Rebekah well knew her brother Laban so highly prized. Laban would then have devoutly exclaimed on Jacob's opening negotiations, 'The thing is altogether from the Lord. I cannot speak to you either bad or good' (24:50). There is my squint-eyed Leah. She will make you a very good wife, but if you prefer Rachel, take her with my blessing."[7]

Deception at the Wedding (29:15-30). Seeing Jacob had come to obtain a wife, Laban proposes that he work for him and asked what wages he desired. Jacob suggested that he work for seven years for the right to marry Rachel, Laban's younger daughter. And Laban agreed.

And so seven years passed. At the end of this period Jacob asked Laban for his wife, and Laban made all the preparations for the usual wedding-feast, which in the East lasts for seven days. At the conclusion of the feast, when Jacob expected Rachel to be brought to the wedding-chamber, Leah was substituted for her sister. The interior of the room was lit only by a small candle, and Jacob did not discover what had happened until the next morning.

He vigorously remonstrated with his father-in-law about the switch, and Laban gave him the lame excuse "It is not the practice in our place to marry off the younger before the firstborn." Why didn't Jacob refuse Leah? To do so would be to disgrace Leah in the eyes of all who lived in Haran and make it impossible for her ever to marry. If a precedent existed whereby the elder daughter was to be married before the younger, why hadn't this condition been made clear to Jacob at the beginning of the seven years? Jacob was beginning to learn what it was like to be cheated of something he deeply desired. To console Jacob Laban said, "Complete the week of this one [namely, Leah], and we will give you the other [Rachel] also for the service which you shall serve with me for another seven years" (29:26-27).

---

7. William H. Thomson, *Life and Times of the Patriarchs, Abraham, Isaac and Jacob* (New York: Funk and Wagnalls, 1912), 186-87. Thomson's comment about Leah being "squint-eyed" is not necessarily accurate. In the Near East having bright, shining eyes is the acme of beauty. Anyone with dull, lack-luster eyes was often overlooked, no matter what their other accomplishments might be.

In this way Laban excused his deception of Jacob and extorted another seven years of labor from him.

But why didn't Jacob tell Laban that his suggestion was unacceptable, and that Rachel should be given to him right away? Then he could take his wives and return to his father Isaac. Rachel was still under her father's control, and Laban could have withheld her from him. In addition, he had not heard from his mother and so had no assurance that Esau's wrath had cooled.

On the eighth day after Leah had become Jacob's wife, Rachel was given to him and their union assuaged in measure Jacob's anger toward his father-in-law.

The experience of Jacob illustrates for us the biblical principle that whatever we sow we also reap (cf. Galatians 6:7; see also Numbers 32:23; 1 Timothy 5:24-25). Laban had deceived Jacob in much the same way that Jacob had deceived his father and brother. And when Laban substituted Leah for Rachel, the deceiver was deceived. This was a painful lesson for Jacob to learn.

God has no favorites, and if His own children wander from the path of righteousness He allows them to suffer in order to bring them back to the straight and narrow way. It is one of the first lessons we learn in the school of obedience.

Partial Fulfillment of the Promise (29:31–30:24). In Near Eastern countries the ability to bear children is looked upon as the *sine qua non* or indispensable qualification of a wife, and the more children a wife is able to give to her husband the more highly she is prized.

Social psychologists have divided families into three basic kinds: child-oriented, home-oriented, and parent-oriented. If we take these basic categories and apply them to what is taught in 29:31–30:24, we find that Jacob's home was detrimental to the development of growing children.

In a *child-oriented* home both parents structure their family around the needs and demands of the children. The husband-wife roles are clearly defined, economic security is highly valued, and community participation is regarded as very important.

The *home-oriented* model is one in which both parents concentrate on developing congenial interpersonal relationships. In this kind of situation the husband-wife roles tend to overlap, family togetherness is stressed, and community participation is of little importance. This is the ideal, and when strengthened by a strong spiritual commitment, the home makes a healthy environment for all concerned.

The *parent-oriented* home is one in which husband and wife concentrate on getting ahead. They are career-oriented, and the family life is built around achievement, personal development, and the acquisition of social skills.[8]

---

8. E. M. Duvall, *Family Development* (Philadelphia: Lippincott, 1971), 78.

The home life of Jacob and his wives was complicated because he had more than one wife, but elements of each of the models may be found in the respective homes that made up his little family. His wives tended to be child-centered, but also were interested in meeting their own needs, and Jacob was interested only in getting ahead.

Leah conceived quickly, and over the next several years she bore Jacob several sons. With the arrival of the first three she hoped that her husband would love her. Unfortunately her love for him was unrequited, and with the arrival of the fourth child she had to console herself with the fact that the Lord knew that she was unloved.

Rachel meanwhile remained childless. As the months were lost in the passage of the years she faced continuous disappointment. One day she expostulated with Jacob, "Give me children, or else I die." This resulted in an angry outburst on the part of her husband, "Am I in the place of God, who has withheld from you the fruit of the womb?" (30:1-2).

Desperately wanting children, and inordinately jealous of her sister, Rachel resorted to a practice that was common in her day, namely, offering her husband a secondary wife whose children would be born on her knees and become hers by adoption.[9] And so Bilhah was given to Jacob as his wife, and in the course of time she bore two sons.

Meanwhile Leah had ceased bearing children and, not to be outdone by her sister, gave Jacob her maid, Zilpah, as a wife; and she also bore two sons.

But what are we to make of the jealousy and rivalry that prevailed in Jacob's home?

An indication of the rivalry between Leah and Rachel is to be found in 30:14-17. Reuben found mandrakes in a field, and brought them to Leah. Mandrakes are a narcotic plant that were esteemed by people of Old Testament times as an aphrodisiac (cf. Song of Solomon 7:13). Rachel learned of this and bargained away Jacob for a night if Leah would give her the mandrakes. Leah agreed. Ironically, Leah conceived that night, whereas the next night Rachel did not.

Finally, God took pity on Rachel and she had a son of her own, Joseph; and with his birth she expressed her thankfulness to God for rolling away her reproach. Then, not content with what she had, she added, "May He add another one."

Dr. William H. Thomson wrote of his own observation of polygamy in Palestine and Syria. "One has to live as I have done in [the Middle East] where polygamy prevails to appreciate what an abiding curse in life it is. Polygamy so lowers the status of woman that in it she can never attain to

---

9. Information also comes from the Ur-Nammu Law Code–the oldest known code of laws–found in Sumer and dating from the 21st century B.C. (Ur-Nammu was the founder and ruler of Ur's Third Dynasty, c. 2044-2007 B.C.). One of the laws propounded by Ur-Nammu allowed for a husband to take a concubine if his primary wife was unable to bear children. Rachel, therefore, relied on this precedent when she gave Bilhah to Jacob.

either dignity or refinement; she is merely a grown up child with the winsome ways of childhood replaced by coarseness of manner or speech."[10]

The relationship of Leah and Rachel account for the number of disagreeable incidents in the story of Jacob and his wives. Dr. Thomson continued: "The earliest recollections of children in such a household is that of cursing and bitterness between mothers, which make their sons and daughters grow up to hate one another, and particularly hate those of the favored wife ... and we know how Joseph, the son of the beloved Rachel, fared with his brothers."[11]

With the birth of Rachel's son, Jacob's thoughts turned to his home. He said to Laban, "Send me away, that I may go to my own place and to my own country. Give me my wives and my children for whom I have served you, and let me depart; for you yourself know my service which I have rendered you" (30:25-26). However, as we shall find, Laban was unwilling for Jacob to leave, and another six or seven years were spent serving his father-in-law.

As we look back over the material we have covered so far, what specific principles stand out?

What Have We Learned? We have already commented on certain practical applications of the text, but one deserves special attention. When the Lord met with Jacob at Bethel He stated that "your descendants shall be like the dust of the

---

10. Thomson, 192.
11. Ibid.

earth, and you shall spread out to the west and to the east and to the north and to the south; and in you and your descendants shall all the families of the earth be blessed" (28:14).

In the birth of Jacob's sons we see the beginning of the fulfillment of God's promise. Later, when Jacob and his family went down to Egypt they numbered 70 persons (46:27), and when they came out of Egypt at the time of the Exodus their fighting men numbered 603,550 (Exodus 38:26; Numbers 2:32). Allowing for each adult male to be married and have only two children, the total number of those who followed Moses in the wilderness exceeded 2,000,000.

God certainly increased the size of Jacob's family. He is always true to His promises! His other promises to Jacob were either fulfilled during Jacob's lifetime or else will be fulfilled in the Millennium.

CHAPTER 3

POETIC JUSTICE

The disparaging term "robber baron" dates back to the 12th century and refers (1) to unscrupulous feudal lords who amassed personal fortunes by using illegal and immoral practices, including excessive taxation and oppression of the poor, to amass their personal fortunes; and to (2) modern-day businesspeople who use unethical practices, including the exploitation of others, to build their own personal wealth.

Though Laban lived centuries before these extortioners, his scandalous practices have labeled him one of the most dishonest men in the Bible. We have only to think of his deceit in respect to Jacob's marriage when he substituted Leah for Rachel, and the way in which he took advantage of Jacob in order to extract seven additional years of service from him, to realize that selfish personal concerns were all that mattered to him. And as we consider his conduct in this present chapter (30:25-43) we see him to be wily and avaricious, unethical and deceitful. He broke an agreement about Jacob's wages as soon as he had agreed to it. He knew well the value of Jacob's services, and with cunning and guile succeeded in persuading him to remain in his employ.

The verses that comprise this section may be divided into two parts: Verses 25-34 are primarily discourse, whereas verses 35-43 are entirely narrative and describe how the Lord blessed Jacob and reversed Laban's fortunes.

The Desire to Return Home. The catalyst that caused Jacob to want to return to his home after fourteen years in Syria was the birth of Rachel's son, Joseph. "Now it came about when Rachel had borne Joseph, that Jacob said to Laban, 'Send me away, that I may go to my own place and to my own country. Give me my wives and my children for whom I have served you, and let me depart; for you yourself know my service which I have rendered you'" (30:25-26).

Jacob's desire to return to Canaan was prompted by several considerations: He had suffered greatly under Laban's hard, selfish, unjust, and perfidious lordship; the birth of Joseph completed his family's circle; and he had an earnest desire to see his aged parents before they died.[12] (In all likelihood he had not heard of his mother's death.)

But why was it necessary for him to ask Laban for his permission to return to Canaan? And why did he ask Laban to give him his wives and children? Laban was the titular head of the family in Haran, and he gave or withheld his consent in all matters pertaining to the family. This was true even though Jacob was now about ninety years of age, and Laban's daughters had been given to Jacob in marriage many years earlier.

But Laban was reluctant to lose Jacob's services. To his request he replied, "If I have found favor in your eyes, please stay. I have learned by divination[13] that the Lord

---

12. George Bush (1796-1859), *Notes on Genesis*, 2 vols. (Minneapolis: Klock and Klock, 1981), II:134.

(*Yahweh*) has blessed me because of you. Name your wages, and I will pay them" (30:27-28).

At first sight it would seem as if Laban was genuinely sorry to hear of his nephew's desire to leave. But it was not regret at the thought of parting with his daughters and grandchildren that caused him to try to keep Jacob in his employ, it was the thought of losing his nephew's profitable service. And his pious use of the name of God should not be construed by us as indicating any genuine Godward relationship. It was nothing less than a cunning means of winning over Jacob to his point of view.

There are many Laban's in the world today. They are not personally pious, but they can and do use appropriate "God language" when it suits their purpose. They can imitate the good in others, especially in their work habits, but they have no personal relationship with the Lord.

In seeking to retain Jacob's services, Laban said, "Name your wages, and I will pay them." Jacob saw therein the means whereby he could secure his family's independence. After fourteen years of service, he had no wealth for his wives and twelve children. It was usual in that age for those to whom the charge of a flock is entrusted to obtain their recompense from the produce or increase of the flock. This Jacob had been denied. When Laban said in effect,

---

13. Divination was a pagan practice involving the flight of birds, examining the entrails of an animal, or some other superstitious rite. Here Laban links what he has done with a supposed belief in Yahweh, the one true God.

"What shall I give you?" (30:31), Jacob saw a means of acquiring legitimate personal wealth.

So he replied, "You shall not give me anything. If you will do this one thing for me, I will again pasture and keep your flock: let *me* pass through your entire flock today, removing from there every speckled and spotted sheep and every black one among the lambs and the spotted and speckled among the goats; and such shall be my wages. So my honesty will answer for me later, when you come concerning my wages. Every one that is not speckled and spotted among the goats and black among the lambs, if found with me, will be considered stolen" (30:31-33).

Laban's response was, "Good, let it be according to your word" (30:34). He readily agreed to this proposal, for he saw a way whereby he could take advantage of his nephew. In the East sheep are generally completely white, and the goats are invariably black. Sheep and goats that are speckled or spotted are rare, and the partly-colored are even rarer. Jacob proposed that all the motley ones born in the future be his, and all the even colored ones be Laban's.

Dr. John Kitto wrote of this transaction, "Laban consented to this arrangement. But the very day that it was completed, he caused to be separated from the flock not only the parti-colored young of the sheep and goats ... but all whether old or young, that had any variation of color in them and placing the small flock thus composed under the charge of his sons ..." (30:34-36).[14] This was a clear violation of the

---

14. Kitto, *Daily Bible Illustrations*, I:296-97.

agreement, and took from Jacob the gene pool from which he might have been able to start a flock of his own.

The Scheme to Secure a Flock of His Own. When Jacob realized what Laban had done he determined upon a strategy that involved selective breeding (30:41-42); and, in the opinion of some, a strategy that produced spotted or speckled young in the pregnant female during gestation.[15] This was the scheme he employed:

> Now Jacob took for himself rods of green poplar and of the almond and chestnut trees, peeled white strips in them, and exposed the white which was in the rods. And the rods which he had peeled, he set before the flocks in the gutters, in the watering troughs where the flocks came to drink, so that they should conceive when they came to drink. So the flocks conceived before the rods, and the flocks brought forth streaked, speckled, and spotted.
>
> Then Jacob separated the lambs, and made the flocks face toward the streaked and all the brown in the flock of Laban; but he put his own flocks by themselves and did not put them with Laban's flock. And it came to pass, whenever the stronger livestock conceived, that Jacob placed the rods before the eyes of the livestock in the gutters, that they might conceive among the rods. But when the flocks were feeble, he did not put them in; so the feebler were Laban's and the stronger Jacob's. Thus the man became exceedingly prosperous, and had

---

15. Cf. Bush, I:137.

large flocks, female and male servants, and camels and donkeys.[16]

Did this strategy work? We have no means of knowing. According to 31:5-13 Jacob ultimately gave the credit for his success to the Lord. And it would seem as if in this way the Lord repaid Laban for his treatment of Jacob (cf. Ezekiel 39:10).

All of this brings us to the point where we ask ourselves, What does this have to do with us?

Looking back we note first of all the tension and bickering that characterized Jacob's home, and we can be thankful that in our country a man is permitted to have only one wife. When this principle is violated by taking a mistress, jealousy and unhappiness are invariably the result, and the children are the innocent witnesses to the spiteful comments and harsh recriminations in their home.

In the Garden of Eden the Lord God provided one woman for the man, and we should be thankful that He, in His profound wisdom, has chosen to spare us from the kind of grief with which Jacob had to contend.

---

16. After finishing this chapter I came across a statement by the late E. M. Blaiklock in his *Bible Characters* (Minneapolis: Bethany House, 1979), 40, "The device which Jacob employed to gain material advantage at Laban's expense was superstition. There is no genetic basis for this practice, and the increase of Jacob's holding over those of Laban must have been due to some providence of God...."

Though the names of some of the children born to Jacob's wives perpetuate the memory of their strife, yet others were named in thankfulness to the Lord for His merciful goodness. We should be careful in the choice of the names of our children.

Second, as we consider Jacob's reliance upon a strategy to produce striped or speckled sheep it seems as if he is afraid to trust God with his affairs. Only as we trust in the Lord with all our heart can He make our paths straight (Proverbs 3:5-6), and lead us in the way He has chosen for us. Laban made his plans, and they failed (Psalm 33:10*b*; Proverbs 15:26; Isaiah 8:10). God blessed Jacob, even though at first he thought that it was his strategy that was giving him success (Proverbs 16:3, 9).

"So [Lord] teach us to number our days that we may present to you a heart of wisdom" (Psalm 90:12).

CHAPTER 4

THE LONG ROAD HOME

A few years ago, while on vacation, my wife and I visited different state parks in the Southwestern United States. In one of these preserved areas we followed signs to a scenic overlook and saw far beneath us a valley with sparkling white water rapids following the course of the canyon. A solitary pillar of rock rose up from the valley floor, and a nearby marker attested to the fact that the column was more than two hundred feet high.

The top of this pillar was flat, and a pair of eagles had found this to be an ideal place to build a rustic nest; and there we saw a mother eagle sitting on her eggs.

It did not take much imagination to realize that when her eaglets hatched out they would be fed by the parents until they were strong enough to survive on their own. Then the parent birds would stir up the nest and nudge their offspring to the edge of the rock platform that had been their home. Fear would probably grip the heart of each fledgling, for their nest of sticks had been the only secure place they had known. However, one by one these baby eagles would be nudged over the edge. As they fell they would flap their wings frantically while their parents watched over them. If one of them was in danger of being dashed on the rocks below, a parent would swop down below it and catch it before it reached the bottom. Then, being borne aloft "on eagles wings" the lesson of independent flight would be repeated.

In a short time each fledgling would master the art of flight, and the exhilaration of soaring heavenward on thermal currents would become a vital part of their everyday experience.

There are times in our lives when we feel the nudge of external and internal stimulae, and face an event that will change our life forever. For example,

- We go off to college, and the challenge of living on our own necessitates that we make adjustments in our lifestyle.

- Later we graduate and embark on a career. For a time all goes well, but a change in upper management reverses our prospects for the future and we conclude that a new sphere of employment is necessary.

- We marry the person of our dreams, and are surprised at how many adjustments we have to make.

- A baby is born into our home, and nothing is ever the same again.

- Death invades our circle—whether within our family or at work—and we face the task of adjusting to the additional responsibilities that are placed upon us.

- One by one our children either marry or go off to college, and we have to contend with the challenge of an empty nest.

- And, in the course of time, we lose our spouse, and have to adjust to life alone.

One person described the human experience as being caught up in a "semipermanent condition of transitionality," as internal and external forces determine our decisions. A simpler way of describing what we experience is: (1) separation, when we leave the old familiar social context; (2) the period of transition or isolation, when we find ourselves caught in a "no man's land" between the old way of being and the new; and (3) when the intended changes have taken place and we find ourselves reintegrated into a new social order on a new basis.

Jacob knew what this was like. Everything in his life was hurrying toward a separation from Laban.

The Crisis (31:1-3). The Lord had blessed Jacob to such an extent that his flocks and herds became the envy of Laban and his sons. The latter attributed his success to craft and deceit, but Jacob had established with Laban the fact that the striped, spotted, and speckled sheep and goats would be his. Jacob had become so rich that he owned vast herds of cattle, and could afford male and female servants.

Laban shared his sons' feelings of envy, and inasmuch as he was used to having his own way and outsmarting his associates, he hardly expected to find himself outwitted by his nephew whose abilities he had exploited for the past twenty years.

The Consultation (31:4-16). Once Jacob had decided to leave Laban's employ he acted promptly. His first step was to consult with his wives.[17] To have them act in unison with him was important. The journey for them would be a long one, beset by many dangers. Much, therefore, depended upon obtaining their acquiescence.

Jacob summoned his wives to meet with him in a field where they could not be overheard. He then recounted to them their father's numerous injustices over the past two decades:

"I see your father's countenance, that it is not favorable toward me as before; but the God of my father has been with me. And you know that with all my might I have served your father. Yet your father has deceived me and changed my wages ten times, but God did not allow him to hurt me. If he said: 'The speckled shall be your wages,' then all the flocks bore speckled. And if he said: 'The streaked shall be your wages,' then all the flocks bore streaked. So God has taken away the livestock of your father and given them to me.... Then the Angel of God spoke to me in a dream, say-

---

17. It is significant that Jacob's secondary wives were not invited to this meeting. No insult was intended. Their absence merely marked them as being wives of lesser rank. No distinction, however, was made between their sons and the sons of Leah and Rachel, for the sons of Bilhah and Zilpah had been legally adopted and were recognized by Jacob as his sons.

ing, 'Jacob.' And I said, 'Here I am.' And He said, 'I have seen all that Laban is doing to you. I am the God of Bethel, where you anointed the pillar and where you made a vow to Me. Now arise, get out of this land, and return to the land of your family'" (31:5-13).

In telling his wives what had transpired he claimed divine approval for his wealth (31:5), recounted God's involvement in granting him riches exceeding Laban's (31:9), and concluded with specific revelation instructing him to return home (31:13).

The true character of Laban is seen from the fact that his daughters sided with Jacob, for they had experienced their father's selfishness and greed, and they were willing to leave their home behind them and go with Jacob to a land they had never seen.

The Flight (31:17-21). Once again Jacob acted with speed. Collecting all he had he set out on his long journey. He did not tell Laban of his plans, for he knew that had he done so Laban would first have tried to dissuade him, and if this did not work, then he would have taken his wives, children, and flocks from him by force.

He did not know that Rachel had stolen her father's household gods.[18] Laban had paid homage to these deities, attributing to them his wealth, and now that his former affluence was visibly diminished, his devotion to these gods had experience a rebirth.

The Pursuit (31:22-24). Jacob seized the opportunity to leave Paddan-Aram when Laban was shearing his sheep three days journey from his home. Making the most of his father-in-law's absence, he moved his slow-moving caravan south as quickly as the newly born lambs and goats would permit.

He had been gone for three days when Laban heard of what had happened. His true intentions at once became evident. He took his kinsmen with him and started off in pursuit of Jacob, intending to bring back by force those whom he regarded as fugitives. But he reckoned without the One who was stronger than all the might he, Laban, could muster. God appeared to him in a dream and sternly warned him to be careful what he said to Jacob (31:24).

It must be remembered that Jacob was God's theocratic representative on earth, and whatever was said or done to him was regarded by the Lord as being said or done to Him.[19] This divine warning was clear proof of what Laban had planned to do when he caught up with Jacob.

---

18. There are many works available on these *teraphim,* see the bibliography in *Unger's New Bible Dictionary* (1988), 490; and J. B. Pritchard's definitive work, *Palestinian Figurines in Relation to Certain Goddesses Known Through Literature* (New Haven, CN: American Oriental Society, 1943), 99pp. The *Ryrie Study Bible,* 54, has a valuable note about *teraphim.*

19. See J. D. Pentecost, *Things to Come,* 433-72.

The Confrontation (31:25-35). After seven days hard travel Laban caught up with his son-in-law. His words to Jacob were a mixture of hypocrisy and exaggeration. His expression of love for his daughters and grandchildren was disingenuous and smacked of affectation (31:26-29). He had many opportunities over the years to show them his love, but the very reverse had been their experience.[20] As Dr. W. H. Griffith Thomas has pointed out, "It is what we are prepared to do for our loved ones while they are with us, not the kind things we say of them after they are gone, that is the real test and genuine measure of our affection."[21]

Not being able to take his daughters and their children by force, Laban then challenged Jacob with the theft of his *teraphim* (31:30*b*). Jacob, of course, was unaware of Rachel's duplicity, and gave Laban permission to search his entire camp, even stating that the one in whose possession these gods were found would be put to death. Because the *teraphim* were supposed to bring fruitfulness, happiness and prosperity, Rachel possibly hoped that they would help her to conceive and have another son.

Laban took Jacob at his word and began going into one tent after another as he searched for his gods. In the course of his ferreting about he came to Rachel's tent. She was as crafty as her father, and had placed Laban's household gods in the camel's saddle. Pretending that she was suffering from severe cramps brought on by her menstrual period, she

---

20. Note Jacob's defense of his actions in verse 31.
21. Thomas, *Genesis*, 286.

sat on her saddle and excused herself from rising when her father entered her tent.

The Vindication (31:36-42). Laban found nothing, and when he emerged from the last tent, it was Jacob's turn to rebuke his inquisitor.

> "What is my transgression? What is my sin that you have hotly pursued me? Though you have felt through all my goods, what have you found of all your household goods? Set it here before my kinsmen and your kinsmen, that they may decide between us two. These twenty years I have been with you; your ewes and your female goats have not miscarried, nor have I eaten the rams of your flocks. That which was torn of beasts I did not bring to you; I bore the loss of it myself. You required it of my hand whether stolen by day or stolen by night. Thus I was: by day the heat consumed me and the frost by night, and my sleep fled from my eyes. These twenty years I have been in your house; I served you fourteen years for your two daughters and six years for your flock, and you changed my wages ten times. If the God of my father, the God of Abraham, and the fear of Isaac, had not been for me, surely now you would have sent me away empty-handed. God has seen my affliction and the toil of my hands, so He rendered judgment last night."

Laban could not respond directly to Jacob's charge and, to try and regain his loss of esteem, suggested that they enter into a bilateral covenant not to do each other any harm in the future.

The Covenant (31:43-55). Jacob set up a pillar as he had done at Bethel, and Jacob's kinsmen erected a mound of stones as a witness to the covenant that would be made. Then they entered into a solemn agreement with the usual sacrifices,[22] and each entreated the Lord to watch between them (for neither trusted the other). It should be noted, however, that Laban still claimed ownership of his daughters and grandchildren, and included in the covenant the fact that if Jacob took additional wives, the property now in Jacob's possession would still belong to Leah and Rachel and their children.

And so the chapter comes to an end with Laban kissing his daughters and their sons, and leaving Gilead for the sheep-shearing of his flocks in Paddan-Aram. But what are we to make of all we have read? 2 Timothy 3:16 explicitly states that "all Scripture is ... profitable for teaching, for reproof, for correction, for training in righteousness; so that the man [or woman] of God may be adequate, equipped for every good work."

This being the case, what do we learn from the information before us?

Enough information has been given about Laban that we do not need to go over it again. What will really be of profit to us is a consideration of God's role in Jacob's affairs.

---

22. H. C. Trumbull, *The Blood Covenant*, 2d ed. (Minneapolis: James, n.d.), 268-69.

God's guidance of Jacob may be traced in Jacob's desire to return home. He had been gone a long time, and apparently had not missed his parents enough to want to see them. Then came the explicit instruction from the Lord to return to Canaan. Inward desire was matched with outward circumstances when he discerned that Laban and his sons were no longer cordially inclined toward him.

Once Jacob had reached a decision in conjunction with his wives, he struck camp and set out for his homeland. And the Lord protected him. His vulnerable caravan was not beset by robbers, and when Laban caught up with him the Lord warned Laban not to do Jacob any harm or even speak harshly to him.

The Lord's sovereign care of each of His servants is now enjoyed by all believers, though not always in the same way (cf. Psalms 37:28; 84:11; 104:27-30; 145:14-16; Romans 8:28). He works all things for the good of each individual believer (Ephesians 1:11).

CHAPTER 5

CONFRONTING AN OLD FEAR

As we grow older some of us confront the memories of our past transgressions. It is as if God, in His all-wise providence, is giving us an opportunity to confess wrongs done long ago and make restitution for the injustices we have committed. Charles William Stubbs (1845-1912) wrote eloquently of his experience.

> I sat alone with my conscience
> In a place where time had ceased,
> And we talked of my former living
> In the land where the years increased;
> And I felt I should have to answer
> The question it put to me,
> And to face the answer and questions
> Through all eternity.
>
> The ghosts of forgotten actions
> Came floating before my sight,
> And things that I thought were dear things
> Were alive with terrible might.
> And this vision of all my past life
> Was an awful thing to face,
> Alone with my conscience sitting
> In that solemn silent place....

Jacob came to such a place. He had faced Laban, and by God's grace his father-in-law had not harmed him nor taken away his family. Laban had then followed the northern route back to his home in Haran. This left Jacob free to proceed south along the eastern bank of the River Jordan. But now he faced a new fear: his brother Esau. He had stolen Esau's birthright twenty years earlier, and he was afraid that Esau might still be intent upon killing him.

By way of encouraging Jacob the Lord sent a company of angels to meet him (32:1). Just how Jacob saw these divine beings–whether in a vision or evident to his physical senses–is not told us. Their presence would have reminded him of Bethel with the angels of God ascending and descending upon the staircase that stretched upward to heaven, and of God's promised protection (Psalm 34:7). We do know that when he saw these angelic beings he was encouraged and exclaimed "This is God's host," and he named the place *Mahanaim,* meaning "double camp" or "two hosts."

And greatly reassured by their presence he journeyed on his way to the brook Jabbok.[23] The Hebrew of 32:3 implies that Jacob had already sent messengers to Esau, for as Dr. George Bush has pointed out, when we compare verses 3 and 6 the messengers returned to Jacob while he was still camping at the brook.[24]

We are not surprised to read that information of Esau's approach with an army of 400 men caused Jacob to become

---

23. *Macmillan Bible Atlas,* #8.

"greatly afraid and distressed" (32:7). His immediate reaction was to revert back to his reliance upon his own abilities, and this shows how little God's assurances of protection had changed his life. As Dr. Merrill F. Unger has shown, "He had learned too little about God at Bethel, and too much about man at Haran."[25] He found it difficult to trust people, and his emotional response gives us a good illustration of how the "fear of man brings a snare" (Proverbs 29:25).

Fear imputes to a person (in this case Esau), place, or thing, two attributes that properly belong to God, namely, almightiness (the power to take away our freedom) and impendency (the power to do us harm). The only antidote to such fear is to place ourselves unconditionally in God's hands and trust ourselves to His sovereign care. Jacob failed to do this. He immediately set about scheming how to placate Esau and still survive with part of his fortune intact. "He divided the people who were with him, and the flocks and the herds and the camels, into two companies; for he said [to himself], 'If Esau comes to the one company and attacks it, then the company which is left will escape'" (32:7-8).

---

24. Bush, *Genesis*, 160. The interval between Laban's departure and Jacob's arrival at the precipitous valley along which the Jabbok runs toward the River Jordan does not allow enough time for Jacob's messengers to go down to Mount Seir and return, if Jacob only sent them when he arrived at the Jabbok. Soon after Jacob and all who were with him arrived at the Jabbok, these messengers returned with disquieting news: Esau was coming to meet him.

25. Unger, *Commentary on the Old Testament*, 82.

With instructions given his servants to put these plans into effect, Jacob turned to God for His blessing (32:9-12). In this respect he did what many of us do today. Whether individually or in a committee, we reach a conclusion about what we believe needs to be done, and then ask the Lord to prosper our decisions.

Jacob called on the Lord to help his plans succeed, and reminded the Lord of what He had promised. He belatedly confessed that he was "not worthy of the least of all God's mercies," and then asked to be delivered "from the hand of ... Esau; for I fear him, lest he come and attack me and the mothers with the children" (32:11).

Then, Jacob went on to remind the Lord of His previous assurances: "You said, 'I will surely treat you well, and make your descendants as the sand of the sea, which cannot be numbered for multitude'" (32:12). We do not find all of these words in God's previous promises, but it is clear that they do represent Jacob's interpretation of the assurances the Lord had given him (cf. 28:15).

After praying to the Lord for His help, Jacob reverted once again to planning how to assuage his brother's anger (32:13-21). He prepared a "gift" of over five hundred animals and divided them into droves: "two hundred female goats and twenty male goats, two hundred ewes and twenty rams, thirty female camels with their young, forty cows and ten bulls, and twenty female donkeys and ten male donkeys." He put them in the care of his servants, each herd by itself, and said to his servants, "Go ahead of me, and keep some space between the herds." He instructed the one in the lead: "When my brother Esau meets you and asks, 'To whom do you belong, and where are you going, and who owns all these animals in front of you?' then you are to say, 'They belong to your servant Jacob. They are a gift sent to my lord Esau, and he is coming behind us.'" And each of Jacob's servants repeated the same statement.

Was all of this preparation necessary? And was his self-abnegation appropriate? If we look ahead to 33:9 we see how Jacob had misread Esau's intentions. Esau intended to invite Jacob and his family to come to Mt. Seir, and the four hundred men were to protect Jacob and his possessions from bandits as they traveled there.

In much the same way, many of our plans are unnecessary. Planning can be appropriate, but it must not take the place of submission to the Lord and His will.

So Jacob's present to Esau passed on before him, while he spent the night alone with his conscience in the camp. His one absorbing thought seems to have been his meeting with Esau. He was alone, and inaction is the most difficult of all situations for a person of Jacob's temperament.

Then we read that "a Man wrestled with him until the breaking of day" (32:24). Dr. Adam Clarke, in his commentary on the Bible, pointed out that the person who wrestled with Jacob was none other than the Lord Jesus Christ, who had assumed human form. Verses 25 and 31-32 show very clearly that this was not a vision or dream, but a physical person.

But why did Jacob's antagonist have to be a person? The answer seems to lie in the difference between the experience of people living then and now. In Old Testament times men and women often experienced physically what we experience spiritually and emotionally.[26] In this they serve to illustrate important spiritual truths. But this does not mean that we spiritualize the text! We interpret it literally, and draw principles from it that apply to our lives.

After hours of strenuous exertion, as the sun began to rise above the distant horizon, and when Jacob's opponent had not prevailed over him, He touched the hollow of his thigh. "Then He said, 'Let me go, for the dawn is breaking.'" But Jacob clung to Him like a boxer that has taken a severe beating, and answered, "I will not let You go unless You bless me." The Lord then asked, "What is your name?" And he said, "Jacob." He said, "Your name shall no longer be Jacob, but Israel; for you have striven with God and with men and have prevailed."

Jacob named the place Peniel, for he said, "I have seen God face to face, yet my life has been preserved." (32:25-31), and though he had to bear the marks of his wrestling the night before, what had happened served as a perpetual reminder for the rest of his life.

---

26. Cf. Abraham's (or Paul's) experience of the Shekinah glory. It was sufficiently real to change the course of his life. And Jacob's wrestling with the Man who came to visit him was just as real and it left him with a pronounced limp.

Now the sun rose upon Jacob just as he crossed over the Jabbok. The fording of the river was made more difficult because he was limping on account of the blow to his thigh. What kind of injury he sustained is difficult to determine. It is not likely that it was complete luxation of the thigh bone, and may mean no more than he received a powerful stroke on the groin (not a touch; for the Hebrew word *naaga'* often signifies to smite with violence).

As Jacob forded the river he looked up and saw Esau coming. But before we consider Genesis 33 we need to look back over the events of this chapter and ask ourselves what the Spirit of God may want us to learn.

One of the first points of application is the reminder that fellowship with God transforms us from our old self into the kind of person the Lord wants us to be (2 Corinthians 3:17-18). But how do we obtain this kind of transformation? Through fasting, nights spent in stoic vigil, observance of the sacraments, penance, or sacrificial service? The answer is simple.

Some years ago a Christian psychiatrist wanted to test the power of the Word of God on people's lives. He chose several conservative institutions and evaluated the incoming students using a series of psychological tests. He found that the results of these tests could be divided into three broad groups—those in Group A had a superior level of mental-emotional health; those in Group B had average mental-emotional health; and those in Group C had a poor level of mental-emotional health. He tested them again in three years and found that those in Group C, who had read their

Bibles regularly had moved up to Group B. Likewise, those in Group B who had read their Bibles regularly had moved up to Group A.[27]

The secret lies in the *use* we make of God's Word (cf. Hebrews 5:11-14).

Second, fellowship with the Lord gives us the presence of mind that enables us to cope with the "Esau's" in our life. It provides us with a balanced perspective. We enjoy insight into the problems we face, pace and patience in grappling with them, and courage in the face of every emergency. We become more than conquerors through Him who loves us (Romans 8:37).

Third, when Jacob came to the end of his struggle with the Lord, he began clinging to Him. His name from birth had been synonymous with cheater or defrauder, but now it was changed to "Israel," one who has power with God and with men. He found that fellowship with the Lord replaced reliance upon human strategies and clever subterfuges. And this parallels the experience of believers today who cease from their own striving and allow the Holy Spirit to control their lives.

---

27. J. D. Woodbridge, ed., *Renewing Your Mind in a Secular World* (Chicago: Moody, 1985), 25-35.

CHAPTER 6

ONE STEP FORWARD, THREE STEPS BACK

In Romans 9:10-13 we come across a strange verse. It takes us back to the time when Rebecca conceived. Before her sons were born God said "Jacob I have loved, but Esau I have hated." The context makes it clear that the issue was *election*, not salvation. Jacob was to be elected to a position of privilege.[28] Yet, as we read Genesis 33:1-17 we find ourselves wondering why the Lord chose Jacob and passed over Esau, for Esau stands out as more honorable than Jacob. In light of this we find it easy to empathize with Charles H. Spurgeon (1834-1892)–who in his day was regarded as the "prince of Bible expositors"–who said that he found it easier to love Esau, for Jacob had little to commend him.

When I was a young Christian I read how the Angel of the Lord wrestled with Jacob and changed his name to Israel. I had earlier read how God had changed Abram's name to Abraham, and this became the name by which he was known from that time onwards. To my surprise I found that Jacob continued to be referred to by the name given him at birth, and only rarely was he called Israel. And in the familiar formula we read of "Abraham, Isaac and *Jacob*," not "Abraham, Isaac and *Israel*." What prevented Jacob

---

28. See Sermon #0239, preached at the New Park Street Chapel, London, January 16, 1859.

from living up to the name the Lord gave him, *viz.*, a "Prince with God"? In my youth I expected the name "Jacob" to disappear from the biblical record and "Israel" to take its place. The reason why this change did not take place is most instructive.

His Meeting with Esau (33:1-11). As the sun rose steadily over the hills Jacob had to face that which he feared most, namely, his meeting with Esau. We would have expected several factors-that the appearance of God to him in Paddan-Aram telling him to return to Bethel; the vision of the company of angels protecting him and all that was his (cf. 2 Kings 6:15-17); God's intervention when Laban planned to harm him; and the events of the night before when he had wrestled with the Angel of the Lord and his name had been changed to Israel–would have been sufficient to reassure him of God's abiding presence and help.

But as he saw clouds of dust rising in the air heralding the approach of Esau and his men his courage failed him. He was filled with fear. Reverting back to his former wily self, he trusted in his cunning and guile rather than in the Lord. He had previously sent several droves of animals to Esau as a gift. Now he divided his family into sections and then crossed over the Jabbok ahead of them. As he limped toward his brother he bowed seven times.[29] Such deference was out of keeping for someone who, the night before, had been made a "prince with God." Had Jacob trusted the Lord

---

29. The significance of this comes from clay tablets unearthed at Amarna as the kind of homage given a king. See Pritchard, *Ancient Near Eastern Texts*, 483-90.

he would have learned that while God does not always remove obstacles from our path, He does give us the ability to deal with them.

As soon as Esau saw his brother he ran toward him, threw his arms about him, and kissed him. And they wept—Esau over joy at seeing Jacob again, and Jacob in relief that his fears had been unfounded. Such a greeting was a far cry from what Jacob had expected. Esau's anger had long since dissipated, and he had become a mighty man, a chieftain, in his own right.

After being introduced to Jacob's family, Esau naturally asked about the droves of sheep and cattle he had met. To his inquiry Jacob responded that they were a present, "to find grace in the eyes of my lord." His servility was both unbecoming and unnecessary. Esau responded by saying that he already had enough wealth. Jacob, however, wanted to purchase Esau's goodwill, and so pressed his brother to accept his gift; and in the end he did.

As we reflect on the meeting between Jacob and Esau we are saddened to note that Jacob was still motivated by fear. He had not learned to trust God. He talked about the Lord (cf. 33:5, 10,11), whereas Esau did not, but though he had been made a prince, he persisted in acting like a pauper.

In reflecting upon Jacob's character I am reminded of a man I worked under before entering the ministry. He was a C.P.A. and ranked second in importance in the company. To my surprise and disappointment I found him to be a pathological liar. He was deceptive and yet adept at concealing from the president the true state of the company's finances.

In time, during an audit, he was found out and left in disgrace.

From Jacob's experience we learn that we should not lift up our eyes and look on those things that trouble us. Instead as we lift up our eyes and look on the Lord we will be able to meet our trials with confidence that He will see us through the problems we face.

The Invitation (33:12-16). Esau was so overjoyed at seeing his brother that he invited him and his family, and all he possessed, to come to Mt. Seir. Jacob declined the proposal by saying, "My lord knows that the children are weak, and the flocks and herds which are nursing are with me. If they are driven too hard, they will die. Please let my lord go on ahead before his servant. I will lead on slowly at a pace which the livestock that go before me, and the children, are able to endure, until I come to my lord in Mt. Seir" (33:13-14). In this exchange Esau stands out as a gracious, loving brother, whereas Jacob is devious and dishonest. As later events show, he had no intention of visiting Mt. Seir.

Esau then offered to leave some of his men with Jacob to guide and protect Jacob and bring him safely to Mt. Seir. Once again Jacob demurred, claiming that there was no need. Esau accepted Jacob's reasoning, and perhaps sorrowfully turned to retrace his steps to his home amid the "rose red hills" that comprised his city. As soon as his brother's dust began to settle Jacob gave instructions for his wives and servants to turn eastward to a place that afterward became known as Succoth ("booths").

Jacob's lies were unworthy of a man of God, and the only other time he saw Esau was when the two of them buried their father Isaac (35:27-29).

At Succoth Jacob wove branches together to form booths for his cattle. Flocks in the East are generally allowed to remain in the open fields by night and day during winter and summer, and are seldom put under cover. The erection of booths by Jacob was unusual, and perhaps the almost tropical climate of the Jordan valley may have rendered some shelter necessary. Or perhaps the booths were for protection against marauding bands who might easily drive off sheep and cattle if they were in an open field.

Jacob called the place where he settled "Succoth," and in time a town was established there. Years later Gideon met with opposition at Succoth when he was pursuing the Midianites (Judges 8:5, 8, 14-16), and still later bronze foundries for making the fine work for the Temple were built here (1 Kings 7:46; 2 Chronicles 4:17). The site is located by some at Tell Ahsas, a mile or more north of the River Jabbok and about nine miles northeast of Damiyeh. Others locate Succoth at Tell Deir 'Alla about two miles north of the Jabbock.

According to the most reliable chronologists, Jacob stayed at Succoth for about ten years. Was this wrong? When the Lord met with Jacob while he was in Paddan-Aram, He said "Return to the land of your fathers and to your relatives, and I will be with you" (31:3). He also identified Himself as the "God of Bethel" and then reminded Jacob that he had anointed a pillar there and also made a vow to the Lord. When in Paddan-Aram the Lord had commanded him to arise, leave the land between the Tigris and Euphrates rivers, and return to the land of his birth (31:13). And when Jacob started out to return to the land of Canaan it was with the expressed intention of seeing his aged father, Isaac (33:18*b*). Actions, however, speak louder than words, and Jacob's actions at Succoth reveal his true motivation.

As we reflect on the contents of these verses, and attempt to draw principles from them for our daily lives, we do so with growing disappointment over Jacob's failure to live up to the privilege that God had given him.

First, we note the awful possibility of failing to live in fellowship with the Lord. Jacob had been elevated to the position of a "prince with God," but he resorted to deception, exposed those whom he professed to love to danger, and lied to his brother. Similarly, external pressures can cause us to focus on ourselves or on material things, with the result that our relationship with Christ suffers (cf. 2 Timothy 4:10).

Scripture contains numerous illustrations of the danger that faces us when we give way to our fears. Peter was with Christ on the Mount of Transfiguration, but this "mountain top" experience did not prevent him from denying Christ on the eve of the crucifixion. In much the same way conventions and deeper life conferences are fine, and we love to have our emotions stirred by some powerful preacher, but these spiritual experiences do not last unless we continue in fellowship with the Lord and grow in a knowledge of the truth. When coldness and apathy begin to characterize our spiritual life we soon cease to pray and it isn't long before we no longer meditate on God's Word. Then worldly interests creep in and the promises we made to the Lord are not fulfilled (cf. 28:19-22). When this happens, we become "disapproved" for future service and lose our reward (cf. 1 Corinthians 9:27; 2 John 8).

Second, there is the matter of priorities. If only Jacob had kept the Lord uppermost in his thoughts and trusted His guidance, the record of his life would have been very different. With trust in God would have come courage to face Esau, victory over the weakness of the flesh, and the speedy fulfillment of his vow. In the same way we often fail because we do not trust the Lord implicitly, and in the wake of distrust comes disobedience. Jacob had ample assurance of God's protection, but when faced with a perceived threat he resorted to duplicitous schemes and an attempt to solve what appeared to be a dangerous dilemma in the energy of the flesh. It is no wonder that toward the end of his life he admitted that "few and unpleasant had been the years of his life" (47:9). How different was Abraham's experience. When he "breathed his last he died in a ripe old age, an old man, and satisfied with life" (25:8).

Let us remember God's promise: We can overwhelmingly conquer through Him who loves us (cf. Romans 8:37; see the context of vv. 35-39).

CHAPTER 7

AN EXPENSIVE PRICETAG

We, today, seldom hear messages on sin, and on the few occasions when we do an individual's or a nation's transgressions are most likely couched in acceptable terms. Sin's wages, however, are very real and we find an illustration of this in Genesis 33:18–35:1. God had told Jacob to go back to Bethel where He had appeared to him, and where Jacob had made a vow (28:10-22).

Instead of obeying the Lord, after meeting with Esau, Jacob chose to go to a place that he named Succoth. There he built a house for himself and booths for his livestock. The patriarchs always had lived in tents, signifying thereby that they were strangers and pilgrims who were looking for a permanent heavenly city (Hebrews 11:13, 16). Jacob chose to depart from this time-honored tradition.

But why did he construct booths for his livestock? The common practice was for sheep and cattle to remain in the open field during the night with shepherds to guard them and ward off any wild beasts.

Jacob was obviously afraid that raiding Bedouin might drive off his livestock and thereby reduce him to poverty. Their typical strategy was to suddenly descend upon a flock or herd, kill the shepherds or herdsmen, and drive off the livestock. Jacob's plan of building booths for the protection of his animals was successful.

After a lengthy stay at Succoth something happened that caused Jacob to leave that region, cross the Jordan River, and take up residence to the east of the city of Shechem.[30] What prompted this move has not been told us, but the fact that the Bible tells us that he arrived in Canaan safe and unharmed implies some sort of threat.

Once the trek from Succoth had been made, Jacob purchased land from the leaders of Shechem and erected an altar. The purchase of land gave him a sense of belonging and entitled his flocks and herds to graze on the nearby hills. And the erection of the altar signified his dependence upon the Lord for help and security.[31]

Genesis 33:19 also mentions a portion of the field (i.e., land suitable for cultivation, cf. 37:7-15; John 4:35), and this, too, Jacob acquired as desirable for agriculture. It probably comprised a considerable part of Wady Sahl, which is "before" or east of Shechem (cf. John 4:12). With these

---

30. The King James Version of 33:18 follows the Samaritan Pentateuch and reads "Jacob came to Shalem, a city of Shechem, which is in the land of Canaan ...." Most modern translations, including the New King James Version, read *salem* as "safely" rather than assume it was the name of another city. The origin of the word *salem* means "whole, safe, in peace," and implies that Jacob and all that he had arrived at Shechem "safe and unharmed."

31. The name Jacob gave the altar, *El-Elhoe-Israel*, "A Mighty God is the God of Israel" confirms this.

AN EXPENSIVE PRICETAG 57

transactions satisfactorily concluded, Jacob settled down to the life of a wealthy "gentleman-farmer."

The Rape of Jacob's Daughter (34:1-17). Jacob, however, was not prepared for the upheaval that occurred. His only daughter[32] Dinah left the relative safety of her father's encampment and went to visit with the "daughters of the land." Whether Jacob felt so secure in his relationship with the Shechemites that he allowed Dinah to go out on her own or whether Dinah stole away from the camp, has not been told us. Not having sisters her own age, she naturally wanted to associate with others who shared her interests. Unfortunately she did not know that in this pagan society a young, unescorted woman was looked upon as "fair game" by whoever found her.

Shechem, the son of Hamor, saw her and was attracted to her. Seizing an opportunity he violently raped her.[33] In spite of his shameful act, he felt a deep attraction for Dinah and asked his father to obtain her for him for a wife (34:4). Dr. Merrill F. Unger wrote: "There can be only condemnation for the crime of Shechem, but the reparation he and his

---

32. The daughter of Leah whose full-brothers were Simeon and Levi. Jacob's sons had girls borne into their homes, but at this point in time Dinah was his only daughter. She had been born when Jacob proposed to Laban that he return to Canaan, and before the six years he served Laban for his flock (30:21, 25-34). Add to this the approximatlly ten years Jacob spent in Succoth, and we can safely say that Dinah was fifteen or sixteen years of age.

father offered [i.e., Shechem's willingness to marry Dinah] was honorable from the viewpoint of human morality."[34]

When Jacob heard of what had happened to Dinah he "held his peace." He was the sheik of his tribe, and (from our point of view) for him to remain silent in the face of such an outrageous act leaves us bewildered. In the ancient Near East, however, with a clan comprising a family by different wives, it is the full brothers upon whom the protection of their sisters devolves. They are the guardians of their sister's welfare and the avengers of her wrongs. It was probably for this reason that Jacob left the redressing of the wrong done to Dinah to Simeon and Levi, and why they took such drastic action. As soon as they heard what had taken place they came back to the camp, and were there when Hamor and Shechem came with Shechem's proposal of marriage (34:8-10).

It was Dinah's brothers, and not her father, who took a prominent part in the negotiations. Hamor was tactful and discrete in his request: "The soul of my son Shechem longs for your daughter; please give her to him in marriage. Intermarry with us; give your daughters to us and take our

---

33. Four times in this chapter the word "defiled" is used to describe Shechem's wicked deed. In 34:2 the Hebrew word means "to humble, to violate." In 34:5, 13, 27 the word means "to make unclean." Pastors and those who have counseled women who have been raped are only too familiar with the feeling of defilement that women feel. Josephus, *Antiquities of the Jews*, 1:21:1, indicates that the rape of Dinah took place at a special Shechemite festival.
34. Unger, *Commentary on the Old Testament*, 84.

daughters for yourselves. Thus you shall live with us, and the land shall be open before you; live and trade in it and acquire property in it" (34:8-10).

The young prince then added: "If I find favor in your sight, then I will give whatever you ask of me. Ask me ever so much bridal payment and gift, and I will give according as you say; but give me the girl in marriage" (34:9-10).

The Treachery of Jacob's Sons (34:18-26). The request of Hamor and Shechem gave Simeon and Levi the opportunity to impose a condition of their own. They stated that it would be impossible for any of their women to be married to an uncircumcised man (34:14-16). Circumcision was a well-known practice among certain races (e.g., Arabs, Moabites, Ammonites, Edomites, Egyptians, et cetera),[35] and so when the need to be circumcised was raised by Dinah's brothers it met with no resistance (34:22-23).

What surprises us is the fact that Simeon and Levi used circumcision–a sign of their covenant relationship with the one, true God–as a pretext to cover their treacherous plan. Their plan was sacrilegious! But why was Jacob silent during these negotiations? True, he could not know of their contemplated treachery, but the negotiations now had entered a different (religious) dimension in which he was *the* leader of his family. His silence is both surprising and disappointing. He could have used this opportunity to speak

---

35. In Canaan the Philistines remained uncircumcised, and for this reason the term "uncircumcised" was constantly used in a derogatory sense.

of his people's unique relationship with the Lord. But he did not.

The Treacherous Actions of Jacob's Sons (34:18-29). The requirements of Simeon and Levi were welcomed by Hamor and Shechem, and accepted by all the mature men of the city (i.e., "all who went out of the gate," 34:24), and they submitted to the rite. Then, on the third day, when they were in pain and their incisions were inflamed, Simeon and Levi took their swords, entered the city and killed every male in it. This included Hamor and Shechem; and they took Dinah from Shechem's house.

After this, Jacob's sons looted Shechem of all its wealth, and took captive the women and children to either serve as their slaves or be sold into slavery (34:28-29).

Jacob's Fear of Reprisal (34:30-31). Throughout these proceedings Jacob appeared passive. Now, however, he responded with reproof of his sons for their actions. "You have troubled me by making me odious to the inhabitants of the land—among the Canaanites and the Perizzites—and since I am few in number, they will gather themselves together against me and kill me. I shall be destroyed, my household and I."

William H. Thomson, M.D., who spent many years as a missionary doctor in Palestine and Syria, explains Jacob's fear. "Blood feuds are common, and were carried out by the 'murdered man's relatives.' If they could not catch the murderer himself, then they could kill some relative of his." Dr. Thomson continued by saying, "I have known such plans of revenge to be nursed for twenty years till a favorable opportunity should occur."[36]

Jacob's sons had slaughtered every male in the city of Shechem, and there probably were many male relatives in the surrounding area–fathers, brothers, uncles, nephews, cousins–who would feel obligated to redress the massacre perpetrated by Jacob's sons. And Jacob's entire family might be annihilated in the process. Once again the Lord intervened, and the "fear of the Lord" made people in the surrounding nations afraid of Jacob and his sons (35:5).

Years later Moses tried to mitigate this savage custom by instituting the Cities of Refuge (Numbers 35:9-34), and regulating what the "avenger of blood" might and might not do.

The Word of the Lord (35:1). After this the Lord said to Jacob, "Go up to Bethel and settle there, and build an altar there to God, who appeared to you when you were fleeing from your brother Esau." And with Jacob's plans having failed at Succoth and Shechem, he did so.

As we review the events of this chapter there are several points that deserve our attention.

One of the first is where we choose to live. We are a mobile society, and sociologists tell us that most families move every five to seven years. What should we look for when we are transferred to a new city? As far as Jacob was

---

36. W. H. Thomson, *Life and Times of the Patriarchs*, 130.

concerned, the fields around Shechem were large and attractive. But what of the pagans living in the area? He may have felt that his experiences with Laban and the people of Haran had equipped him with all the knowledge he needed to be able to handle those living in Shechem. But he was wrong!

When relocation is forced upon us, the choice of a neighborhood in which to live and suitable schools for our children are vital issues and demand careful consideration. And what of our family's spiritual welfare? Are there any sound, Bible-believing churches in the area where our sons and daughters can meet with others of their same age? Or is the church in the area a fashionable one where either formalism or intellectualism is the accepted norm? These and other matters need to be weighed carefully before we expose our children to an unhealthy and unwholesome environment.

Second, Jacob further illustrates for us how a secular attitude can overcome our spiritual commitments, unless we are well-grounded in our faith. When some external threat invades the inner sanctum of our lives we are tempted to give way to human strategies. This tendency is also prevalent among those who once "ran well," but now have yielded to worldly pressures.

Jacob had imbibed a secular attitude, and this prevented him from bearing an effective witness to the one true God. "The Canaanites were then in the land;" they saw Jacob build an altar, but he seemed content to live among them and trade with them, and the "god" whom he professed to worship did not appear to be any different from the gods of their Canaanite pantheon.

Third, as believers in Christ we are called upon to be lights in a dark world. We have been sent into the world to witness to the truth. It is our responsibility to mirror the excellencies of the Lord Jesus in a winsome way as we sanctify Christ as Lord in our hearts. In this way we will be ready in a gentle and reverent way to make a defense to everyone who asks us to give an account for the hope that is in us (cf. 1 Peter 3:15). There is no evidence that Jacob did this.

Jacob illustrates for us the painful path of disobedience to the revealed will of God, and the loss of his testimony that resulted from his noncompliance with God's revealed will.

CHAPTER 8

THE ALL-SUFFICIENT ONE

The late J. Robert Ashcroft once remarked, "All heaven is waiting to help those who will discover the will of God and do it." When Jacob fled from his brother Esau and spent the night at Bethel, the Lord appeared to him and made a covenant with him. Jacob responded by making a vow to the Lord. Now, after a lengthy stay in Paddan-aram, the Lord commanded him to "go up to Bethel," build an altar there, and perform the vow he had made.

Jacob did indeed leave Paddan-aram, but he did not return to Bethel. Instead, after meeting with Esau, he spent ten years at Succoth. When compelled to leave there, he went to Shechem completely bypassing the main road that led to Bethel.

While Jacob was in Shechem the Lord appeared to him again and said, "Arise, go up to Bethel and dwell there; and make an altar there to God, who appeared to you when you fled from the face of Esau your brother." It was over thirty years since this vow had been made (28:20-22), and though the conditions of God's covenant had been exactly and completely fulfilled, the vow Jacob had made was as yet unpaid. The fact that Jacob had delayed to make good his promise shows his spiritually lax condition. He appears to have been indifferent to the true nature of his offense.

Vows in biblical times were entirely voluntary but once made, they were regarded as compulsory, and evasion of performance of them was held to be contrary to true spirituality (cf. Numbers 30:2; Deuteronomy 23:21; Ecclesiastes 5:4). If a person in a dependent position made a vow, (such as an unmarried daughter living in her father's home, or a wife (even if she afterward became a widow), if in the first case her father, or in the second her husband, heard the vow and disallowed it, it was void.

A worship who that had freely undertaken a vow (i.e., in which he had pledged himself before God to perform a specific deed or to dedicate something to the Lord) was on no account to draw back from his promise but conscientiously to carry it out. Otherwise a slight would be put upon God and a stain left upon the conscience of the worshiper (cf. Deuteronomy 23:21-23; Ecclesiastes 5:5; Psalm 50:14; Nahum 1:15).

Jacob had become aware of the fact that certain members of his family were worshiping idols. The first thing to be done, therefore, was for those thus engaged to renounce their worship of the *teraphim* (i.e., idol deities). These objects of their devotion were incompatible with the worship of the Lord. Jacob, therefore, commanded them to put away the foreign gods that were among them, purify themselves, and change their garments.

So they gave Jacob all their foreign gods, and the earrings which were in their ears; and Jacob hid them under the oak tree which was near Shechem (35:1-4). This was to be followed by purifying themselves and putting on clean clothing. Dr. Warren W. Wiersbe has pointed out that "in Scripture, washing the body and changing one's clothes

THE ALL-SUFFICIENT ONE 67

symbolized a new beginning,"[37] and this act finds its counterpart today in confession of sin and a renewing of one's mind (1 John 1:9; Romans 12:1-2).

Jacob had evidently known of the pagan practices of members of his family, but until now he had done nothing to stop it. Even his beloved Rachel had been guilty of idolatry (cf. 31:19).

As they journeyed toward Bethel "there was a great terror upon the cities which were around them, and they did not pursue the sons of Jacob" (35:5). The Hivite tribe of which the Shechemites were a part were closely allied to the Perizzites and other races in Canaan, and these kindred people would regard the destruction of the Hivites in a very personal way. It would have been natural for them to take up a blood feud, and prosecute it to the bitter end. Had they done so, Jacob and all who were with him would have been massacred. The fact that these tribes did not attack Jacob and his slow-moving flocks and herds reminds us of Proverbs 16:7 where we read that when a man's ways please the Lord, He makes even his enemies to be at peace with him. And so Jacob's family and their servants passed by unharmed.

"So Jacob and all the people with him came to Luz (that is, Bethel) in the land of Canaan. There he built an altar, and he called the place *El Bethel*, because it was there that

---

37. W. W. Wiersbe, *The Bible Exposition Commentary: Pentateuch* (Colorado Springs: Victor, 2001), I:36.

God revealed himself to him when he was fleeing from his brother" (35:6-7). In Shechem Jacob had built an altar that he called *El-Elohe-Israel*, "God the God of Israel" (33:20). To be sure it was intended to honor the Lord, but the name he gave it also honored him. Now, in Bethel, emphasis upon himself had been entirely replaced by thoughts of the Lord. He was now thinking of God alone, hence the name "God of Bethel."

As Jacob recalled to mind God's former blessings, and his altar (testifying to his worship of the one true God) and sacrifices, it indicated his renewed *dedication* to the Lord. Though "dedication" is very much a part of our Christian vocabulary, the idea is rooted in the Old Testament. It involves (1) a commitment of ourselves to the Lord (Psalms 10:14; 22:8), or (2) devoting things to His service (Psalms 31:15; 37:5; Proverbs 16:3; etc.).[38]

The usual words used to describe dedication are *hanak*, "to discipline, dedicate, train up," *hanuka'*, "consecration," and the idea of dedication and/or consecration is often associated with *qadash*, which in the New Testament is referred to as "sanctification, holiness." From this brief survey it will readily be seen that Jacob's rededication of himself (probably symbolized by a whole burnt offering) was vitally important.

---

38. See H. F. Vos' discussion in his *New Illustrated Bible Manners and Customs* (Nahsville: Nelson, 1999), 95-98.

It is not recorded that Jacob built himself a house in the vicinity of Bethel. Probably Bethel did not satisfy the requirement of a permanent settlement. Visitors to Bethel reported that the neighborhood is barren, bleak, and stony. The bare hill-tops and narrow valleys might furnish sufficient sustenance for a moderate number of sheep and goats and camels, but there would have been little pasture for horned cattle or donkeys. It is true that Abraham had lived there, together with Lot his nephew, when he came from Egypt (13:3-18), but the strife between their herdsmen soon showed the incapacity of the district to produce sufficient food for their flocks and herds. And soon after Lot's withdrawal, Abraham was forced to move to the Negev (or Southland). We may presume, therefore, that Jacob experienced similar difficulties. He had with him, not only the livestock that he had acquired in Haran, but the sheep and oxen and donkeys taken from the Shechemites (34:28).[39]

With this brief resume of events, we ask ourselves, "What lasting principles can we glean from these verses?"

We first learn of God's unfailing faithfulness. In spite of the fact that Jacob had lived out of fellowship with the Lord during all the time he was in Paddan-aram and Succoth and Shechem, God had not forgotten him. Outwardly it appeared as if the Lord had left him entirely alone. In a variety of different ways, however, He had protected Jacob

---

39. Cf. G. Rawlinson, *Isaac and Jacob, Their Lives and Times* (London: Nisbet, 1890), 130.

and even "stirred up his nest," until at last he acquiesced and said, "I will arise and go to Bethel."

The older we grow the more we become impressed with the long-suffering love of God. Years ago, when I was in my early teens, we used to sing a chorus:

> I've set my feet on God's road
> And never will I drift or roam.
> Tho' I'm often weary I'll travel
> Till I reach my home.
> Ten thousand foes may surround me
> To turn me from the right,
> But God's great arms are around me;
> His arms of love and light.

In spite of the fact that we lived in a God-less city, few of us knew of the difficulties we would face as we tried to live for Christ. This chorus served to fix our eyes on the goal of serving Christ effectively knowing that He would help and care for us.

Second, the experience of Jacob alerts us to the danger of a spiritual laissez-faire attitude that robs us of the joy of the Lord and minimizes our effectiveness. Even though Jacob had been granted a unique experience when he had seen a stairway reaching from earth to heaven and God spoke to him directly, we have been granted a similar privilege. We have God's Word and can receive instruction from it by reading it every day.

When Jacob lived in the house of Laban all his thoughts were of Rachel, and it is probable that he hardly realized the spiritual laxity that was taking place in his life. A man should love his wife, but she should share his devotion to the Lord, not replace it. If his affections are such that she eclipses his love for the Lord, then he becomes guilty of a form of idolatry.

There are many different kinds of idols—making a reputation for ourselves, amassing a fortune, or becoming preoccupied with some pastime that is detrimental to our spiritual growth—are all forms of idolatry and must be judged and put away. God-appointed relationships are not wrong, but we need to keep the Lord uppermost in our affections.

An unknown writer penned the following:

I had walked life's way with an easy tread,
Had followed where comforts and pleasures led,
Until one day in a quiet place
I met the Master face to face.

With station and rank and wealth as my goal,
Much thought for my body but none for my soul,
I had entered to win in life's mad race,
When I met the Master face to face.

I met Him and knew Him and blushed to see
That His eyes full of sorrow were fixed on me,
And I faltered and fell at His feet that day
While my castles melted and vanished away.

Melted and vanished, and in their place,
Naught else did I see but the Master's face;
And I cried aloud, "Oh make me meet
To follow the steps of Your wounded feet."

My thought is now for the souls of men;
I have lost my life to find it again,
E'er since one day in a quiet place
I met the Master face to face.

Third, God's call to renewal did not absolve Jacob of his vow. He had promised that the Lord would be his God. After years of waywardness he needed to acknowledge his delinquency, confess his spiritual apathy, renew his devotion to the Lord, and put right whatever he could. His actions provide a pattern of renewal for us. Only then can we sing:

O Jesus, I have promised to serve You to the end,
   Be forever near me, my Master and my Friend;
I shall not fear the battle if You are by my side,
   Nor wander from the pathway if You will be my Guide.

CHAPTER 9

RENEWAL OF THE PROMISE

Above the door of a hospice in Whittier, California, is a plaque. It cannot be seen by those entering the building, but it breathes comfort to those who leave. It reads:

God saw that he was getting tired and a cure was not to be.
So He put His arms around him and whispered
"Come home with Me."
With tearful eyes we watched him suffer
And saw him fade away;

Although we loved him dearly, we could not make him stay.
A golden heart stopped beating, a determined spirit was at rest,
God broke our hearts to prove to us--He only takes the best!
–Author unknown.

The Death of a Beloved Servant. According to 35:8 Deborah, Rebekah's nurse, died at Bethel while Jacob and all who were with him were living there. She was buried below the town under an oak tree, which was named *Allonbacuth* ("oak of weeping").

Nurses held a high and honorable place in ancient times, and especially in the East (2 Kings 11:2), where they were often the principal members of the family (2 Chronicles 22:11).[40] Many years earlier Deborah had accompanied Rebekah from the house of Bethuel (24:59) when her

---

40. Cf. Homer, *Odyssey*, 1:429; Virgil, *Aenid*, 7:2.

mistress had left Paddan-aram to be married to Isaac, but she is mentioned by name only on the occasion of her burial.[41]

It is probable that after Rebekah's death Deborah stayed with Isaac. But when she heard that Jacob was at Bethel she went to be with the boy she had helped raise since his birth.

Jacob's loving treatment of this elderly servant shows his genuine affection for her. The death of a servant would not ordinarily occasion much regret, but the passing of Deborah was different. Jacob's family went to the place of her interment and wept over her grave. Those who grieved her passing were not those with whom she had spent most of her life, but they had cared for her in her old age, and in their sorrow they recalled her quiet, graceful spirit, as well as her kind and efficient service.

As a pastor I have conducted numerous funerals and grave side services. Those who mourn the loss of a loved one are generally preoccupied by two questions: "Can we be sure that thee is there life after death?" and "Where is -- now?"

Scripture emphasizes the fact that death is separation not a cessation. The general teaching of God's Word is that human beings are not only physical but also spiritual. Accordingly, death is not the end of human existence, but a

---

41. That Rebekah was dead may validly be inferred from the fact that her name is omitted in 35:27, though when she died is not specified.

change of place in which the deceased's conscious existence continues (John 5:25, 28-29). Death is the result of sin (Romans 6:23), but through faith in the atoning work of the Lord Jesus believers are given eternal life (John 5:24).

Because going to heaven is vitally connected with the death *and* resurrection of Christ, the righteous dead in Old Testament times went to Paradise (Luke 23:43, also called "Abraham's bosom" in Luke 16:20, 22). According to the story the Lord Jesus told there are two sections to Paradise. The one is a place of peace and blessing, and the other is a place of torment called Hades (Luke 16:26).

Once the Lord Jesus rose from the dead and ascended into heaven Paradise was emptied and those who were there were translated into heaven (cf. 2 Corinthians 12:4). Now, following Christ's resurrection, all who have placed their trust in Him go immediately into His presence when they die (2 Corinthians 5:8).

The Renewal of a Promise. After Jacob had learned of the death of his mother and buried Deborah, the Lord appeared to him and renewed the promise He had made to him many years earlier (35:9-15).

The Bible's critics claim that the covenant in these verses is a different version of the covenant of 28:10-22 and comes from a different manuscript source. It should be noted, however, that this repetition of the covenant differs in time and in specifics from the covenant made with Jacob when he saw the staircase stretching from earth to heaven. On the former occasion God appeared to him when he was en route to Paddan-aram, whereas on this occasion Jacob had come from Paddan-aram (35:9). Only the place was the same. Furthermore, God met with Jacob after the solemn sacrificial rites were over (35:10-12). On Jacob's first visit to Bethel he had no animal with him to offer as a sacrifice.

By appearing to Jacob the Lord testified to His acceptance of Jacob's sacrifice, and then He honored Jacob by reiterating his change of name. He said to him "Your name is Jacob; you shall no longer be called Jacob, but Israel shall be your name"--thus confirming the new *nomen* given Jacob at Peniel (cf. 32:28). Then the Lord continued His pledge to fulfill the conditions of the covenant even to the remote future. But this was not all. God added,

"I am *El Shaddai* [God Almighty];[42]
Be fruitful and multiply;
A nation and a company of nations shall come from you,
And kings shall come forth from you.
The land which I gave to Abraham and Isaac,
I will give it to you,
And I will give the land to your descendants after you."

In this reiteration of the blessings of the covenant the Lord further stated that Jacob would be the father of a great nation and that kings would be among his descendants. Then He confirmed the gift of the land. It had already been

---

42. The "all-sufficient One" (35:11), who is able to make good His promise in due time, and to support Jacob and provide for Him both now and in the future.

promised to Abraham and Isaac, and now this promise was renewed to Jacob.

These promises have far-reaching significance, for they will find their ultimate fulfilment in the Lord Jesus Christ when He receives the Kingdom from His Father and reigns over the nations of the world.

It is comforting for us to know that God also restored Jacob to a place of blessing. He now had a new beginning. But what of the thirty-plus years during which he had lived for himself? What kind of a testimony did he have among those with whom he lived and labored in Paddam-aram?

Robert Whitaker (1863-1944), an American clergyman, historian, and poet, admonished all of us when he wrote:

Live for something, have a purpose,
    And that purpose keep in view;
Drifting like a helmless vessel,
    Thou canst ne'er to life be true.
Half the wrecks that strew life's ocean,
    If some star had been their guide
Might have now been riding safely.
    But they drifted with the tide.

Live for something, and live earnest,
    Though the work may humble be,
By the world of men unnoticed,
    Known alone to God and thee.
Every act has priceless value
    To the architect of fate;
'Tis the spirit of thy doing

> That alone will make it great.
>
> Live for something—God and angels
> Are thy watchers in the strife,
> And above the smoke and conflict
> Gleams the victor's crown of life.
>
> ....

Solomon confirmed the wisdom of this sentiment when he said, "Whatever your hand finds to do, do it with all your might; for there is no activity or planning or knowledge or wisdom in *Sheol* (i.e., the grave)[43] where you are going" (Ecclesiastes 9:10). And the Apostle Paul reiterated the same thought when he wrote, "Whatever you do, do your work heartily, as for the Lord rather than for men, knowing that from the Lord you will receive the reward of the inheritance, [for] it is the Lord Christ whom you serve" (Colossians 3:23-24).

---

43. For a full discussion, see Holloman, *Kregel Dictionary of the Bible and Theology*, 499-500.

CHAPTER 10

ON THE ROAD AGAIN

H. V. Morton was regarded as one of the greatest travel-writers of the Twentieth Century. He visited many parts of the Middle East, and on one occasion, while standing near a well in Palestine, he saw a young girl as she came to draw water. In typical fashion she was carrying a waterpot on her shoulder. Morton wrote "She was in that brief loveliness of youth which vanishes from an Arab maid almost as one watches. At twenty she is often middle aged; at thirty-five a wrinkled grandmother. But in her teens she sometimes justifies the rhapsodies of the Song of Songs and, standing for a moment against the ageless background of the desert, typifies in a remarkable manner the women of the Bible ... Ruth, Rachel, or Rebekah."[44]

Rachel was married to Jacob. Students of human nature agree that Jacob's character was ruined by his mother, Rebekah. He was her favorite son, and his love affair with Rachel can best be described as a quest to find another woman exactly like his mother. In this respect Rachel and Rebekah were astonishingly alike, and in the changes that took place during their lives less admirable qualities became apparent.

---

44. H. V. Morton, *Women of the Bible* (London: Methuen, 1940), 3.

Jacob had been tricked into marrying Rachel's older sister, Leah, and only married Rachel a week later. Leah loved Jacob, but there is no indication in the Bible that Rachel loved him as much. In fact, even after her marriage to Jacob, she remains one of those women with nothing to commend her but her beauty.

The Birth of Benjamin. In 35:16-20 we have the continuing saga of Jacob and his family. He decided to move again, and journeyed south from Bethel toward the little village of Ephrath (that later became known as Bethlehem). En route Rachel, who was pregnant, began to experience severe labor pains, and the midwife who was attending her tried to encourage her by saying, "Do not fear; you will have this son also." Rachel, however, died in childbirth. As her soul was departing she called his name Ben-oni, meaning "son of my sorrow." Jacob would not allow this, and changed his name to Benjamin, "son of my right hand."

Jacob's sorrow must have been very great at the loss of his beloved Rachel. All we are told is that he buried her and set a pillar over her grave.[45] When we compare the passing of Rachel with the death of Deborah, there is no record of anyone weeping at Rachel's grave side. Apparently the easy charm of her youth vanished into an envious and irritable middle-age, for she became bitter, envious, quarrelsome and petulant.

---

45. See Robinson, *Biblical Researches*, I:218, 469; and Thomson, *The Land and the Book*, 406.

Jacob's Name Renewed. It is surprising to read that after Rachel's death "*Israel* journeyed on ...." Matthew Henry states that "The historian does him this honour here because he bore the affliction with such admirable patience and submission to Providence," but the great Bible expositor does not cite the source of his quotation. What is probable is that Rachel was a spiritual stumbling block to her husband, and he only began to walk with the Lord as a "prince with God" after her death.

As Jacob journeyed on he came to the "tower of Eder," or "tower of the flock" (Micah 4:8). It is supposed that this tower was about a mile from Bethlehem, and to have been a watchtower for shepherds (35:21).

The Sin of Reuben. Not content with the locality, Jacob journeyed on and pitched his tent beyond the tower of Eder. "Now it came about while Israel was dwelling in that land, that Reuben went in and had sexual relations with Bilhah, and Israel heard of it" (35:22).

Reuben was Jacob's oldest son (29:31-32), and was most likely a young man in his mid-thirties. Bilhah had been Rachel's maid whom she gave to Jacob as a wife in order that she might adopt Bilhah's children as her own. Now, with Rachel having died, Reuben realized that there was no one to protect Bilhah, and so took the opportunity to have sexual intercourse with her.

But why did Reuben do this? Surely he had a wife or wives of his own. And seeing the text does not indicate that Reuben raped her, we may legitimately presume that Bilhah willingly acquiesced.

With Jacob's grief over the loss of Rachel, Reuben possibly believed that his father was no longer capable of giving leadership to the extended family. Taking his father's wife, therefore, was an open declaration on his part that he now considered himself head of the clan.[46]

When Jacob learned of what had happened, he took away forever Reuben's right to lead the family (cf. 44:3-4; comp. vers. 8-10). But what of Bilhah? What could she possibly gain by acquiescing to Reuben's advances? If Reuben had been successful in asserting his right to lead the clan, she would have become the "No. 1 wife" of the new sheik.

The Sons of Jacob. In 35:22*b*-26 we are given the register of Jacob's twelve sons. But why are they mentioned now? The answer seems to be that the future history of the family deals primarily with the sons of Jacob as the fathers of the twelve tribes of Israel. They are listed not in the order of their birth, but according to their maternal parentage.

---

46. This was an old, well-established custom. When David succeeded king Saul, he was given Saul's wives, thus establishing his right to rule the northern tribes (1 Samuel 12:8). After Abner had sex with King Saul's concubine, Saul's son Ishbosheth realized that Abner was laying claim to the throne (2 Samuel 3:6-11). Later, when David was forced to vacate the city of Jerusalem, Absalom took his father's concubines, indicating thereby that he was the new king in Jerusalem (2 Samuel 16:20-23). And after David's death, when Adonijah asked that Abishag be given to him as a wife, Solomon knew that back of the request was a subtle move to assert his right to sit on David's throne (1 Kings 2:13-25).

The Bible has always had its detractors, and when commenting on these verses some of them are quick to point out that Jacob's sons were not all born in Paddan-aram, for Benjamin (as we have just learned) was born in Canaan, near Bethlehem.

The answer to this carping criticism is not hard to find. According to common usage, when the majority of people came from one place the usual practice was to link them all together.[47]

Jacob's sons are again listed in Genesis 49:1-27. It is generally believed that this chapter contains the "blessing" Jacob gave his children before he died. Verse 1 starts with a summary statement. This is what Jacob said, "Gather together, that I may tell you what shall befall you in the last days: Gather together and hear, you sons of Jacob, and listen to Israel your father."

Then he proceeded to speak about each of his sons in turn:

"Reuben, you are my firstborn, my might and the beginning of my strength, the excellency of dignity and the excellency of power. [You are] unstable as water, you

---

47. Examples of this are found in the New Testament as well. For example when the Lord Jesus said to His disciples, "You will sit on twelve thrones judging the twelve tribes of Israel" (Matthew 19:28), there were only eleven disciples, for Judas had hanged himself. And when the Lord Jesus appeared to the twelve after His crucifixion, there were only eleven, for Judas was dead. Other examples could be cited.

shall not excel, because you went up to your father's bed, and defiled it.

"Simeon and Levi are brothers; instruments of cruelty are in their dwelling place. Let not my soul enter their council; let not my honor be united to their assembly; for in their anger they slew a man, and in their self-will they hamstrung an ox. Cursed be their anger, for it is fierce; and their wrath, for it is cruel! I will divide them in Jacob and scatter them in Israel.

"Judah, you are [the one] whom your brothers shall praise; your hand shall be on the neck of your enemies; your father's children shall bow down before you. [You are] a lion's whelp; from the prey, my son, you have gone up. He bows down, he lies down as a lion; and as a lion, who shall rouse him? The scepter shall not depart from Judah, nor a lawgiver from between his feet, until Shiloh comes; and to Him shall be the obedience of the people....

"Zebulun shall dwell by the haven of the sea; he shall become a haven for ships, and his border shall adjoin Sidon.

"Issachar is a strong donkey, lying down between two burdens; he saw that rest was good, and that the land was pleasant; he bowed his shoulder to bear a burden, and became a band of slaves.

"Dan shall judge his people as one of the tribes of Israel. Dan shall be a serpent by the way, a viper by the path, that bites the horse's heels so that its rider shall fall backward...."

"Gad, a troop shall tramp upon him, but he shall triumph at last.

"Bread from Asher shall be rich, and he shall yield royal dainties.

"Naphtali is a deer let loose; he uses beautiful words.

"Joseph is a fruitful bough, a fruitful bough by a well; his branches run over the wall. The archers have bitterly grieved him, shot at him and hated him. But his bow remained strong, and the arms of his hands were made powerful by the hands of the Mighty God of Jacob....

"Benjamin is a ravenous wolf. In the morning he shall devour the prey, and at night he shall divide the spoil.[48]

"These are the twelve sons of Israel, and this is what their father spoke to them."

Finally ... (35:27-29). Finally, after many digressions, Jacob arrived in Mamre and went to see his aged father who was living in Hebron. The biblical writer then closes with

---

48. See Robert S. Candlish's *Exposition of Genesis* (1842). This work has been reprinted many times.

the death of Isaac, and the impression left upon the reader is that Jacob no sooner saw Isaac than his father expired. Such a view distorts the sequence of events.

The sacred historian's purpose is to pass on to the history of Jacob's sons. Before he can proceed, however, there are two other matters that must be treated. One of these is the death of Isaac, and the other is a brief history of the life of Esau. Then, with both men having been dismissed from the biblical record, the way is open for a discussion of the fortunes and misfortunes of Jacob's family.

We have no means of knowing what memories coursed through Jacob's mind as he went to see his father. Did he recall happy times together, and his mother's strong influence on their lives? And did he experience feelings of shame as he recalled how he had lied to his father and cheated his brother?

Jacob's children would have been keenly interested in meeting their grandfather and the patriarch of their family, and Isaac may have recalled that day more than thirty years earlier when he had bestowed his paternal blessing on Jacob and sent him to Paddan-aram to obtain a wife for himself. Little did he realize then that his son would return with twelve sons and numerous grandchildren. And how his heart must have quickened as he heard of all that Jacob had done and how the Lord had blessed him.

Isaac lived to be 180 years old. He was 137 at the time Jacob left to go and live with Laban. Jacob had been gone for between 35 and 40 years, and so the time for father and son to enjoy each other's company was limited to at most eight years.

As Isaac's days on earth drew to a close, a messenger was sent to Edom with a message for Esau. He hurried to his father's bedside, and Isaac had the joy of being reunited with his favorite son before he died. After he passed on to be with Abraham and the other godly people in Paradise, he was buried by Jacob and Esau in the Cave of Machpelah.[49]

Just what interaction took place between Jacob and Esau during the time they were together has not been told us. All we know is that this was the last time they saw each other.

Now, as we pause to review the events of this chapter we note that death is inevitable. Happy are those individuals who die in the confident assurance that their sins have been forgiven. But God does not forget us in our sorrow. We who are left behind have to learn with the Lord Jesus what it is like to be "made perfect through suffering."

The pain of loss is very acute, and it takes time for us to recover; but help is available.[50]

"Therefore we do not lose heart, but though our outer man is decaying, yet our inner man is being renewed day by

---

49. See Thomson, *The Life and Times of the Patriarchs*, 145-56.
50. The *process* of resolving the pain that accompanies the loss of a loved one has been described in *Through the Valley of Tears* (Eugene, OR: Wipf and Stock, 1987), 216pp.

day. For our momentary, light affliction is producing for us an eternal weight of glory far beyond all comparison, while we look not at the things which are seen, but at the things which are not seen; for the things which are seen are temporal, but the things which are not seen are eternal" (2 Corinthians 4:16-18).

CHAPTER 11

LOVE'S INDISCRETIONS

A few years ago I attended a seminar at which a well-known authority on marriage and family life was the featured speaker. On being introduced he strode toward the podium amid thunderous applause. When the clapping and cheers subsided the speaker began his presentation with words I shall never forget:

"The greatest misfortune that can befall a child is to have parents."

At first I thought, "How can a child be born unless he has parents?" Then a deeper truth began to make its impact on me, and I remembered words I had read a long time ago:

If a child lives with criticism, he learns to condemn.
If a child lives with hostility, he learns to fight.
If a child lives with ridicule, he learns to be shy.
If a child lives with shame, he learns to feel guilty.
If a child lives with tolerance, he learns to be patient.
If a child lives with encouragement, he learns confidence.
If a child lives with praise, he learns to appreciate.
If a child lives with fairness, he learns justice.
If a child lives with security, he learns to have faith.
If a child lives with approval, he learns to like himself.[51]

Jacob showered special favors on Joseph to the exclusion of his other sons. He had seen firsthand the effects of jealousy on the part of his wives, and this trait had been passed onto their children. Yet this did not stop him from showing partiality toward Joseph.

It would have been natural for Jacob to keep Joseph close to him, even before Rachel died, but with her passing his bias toward Joseph was intensified. The result was predictable. Joseph's brothers resented him, and in time their hatred knew no bounds (37:1-36).

The death of Isaac had established Jacob as the acknowledged head of the tribe. Abraham's and Isaac's long-term residence in central and southern Canaan had given the family certain important rights. At different times both Abraham and Isaac had resided in Hebron--a town in the mountains of Judah, about three thousand feet above the Mediterranean Sea--and Jacob appears to have made it his chief residence (37:14). Hebron was central to the choicest pasture land in the Negev or Southland.

According to Dr. J. Cunningham Geikie who recorded his observations of the region, "Its great reservoirs, probably already excavated [at the time of our story], supplied abundant water; the hillsides of its valleys were noted for their vines; olive trees clothed many slopes; and there was a fair amount of soil suitable for the growth of barley and lentils. The short herbage of the hills furnished the best possi-

---

51. Dorothy Nolte's wise aphorisms were published in the *Torrance Herald*, California, in 1954.

ble pasture for sheep, and the shrubs and bushes which abound afford the food which is most coveted by goats."[52]

Jacob seems to have remained peacefully in Hebron while his sons were scattered over much of Canaan with his flocks and herds. So many were their livestock that the Negev from Bethlehem to Beersheba was considered their unofficial grazing land. They also had a possession in Shechem and, as occasion required, fed their father's livestock on its rich plain (37:12). They lived on friendly terms with the people who regarded Jacob as one of the most prosperous and powerful sheiks of his day.

Though outwardly Jacob's family appeared united, inwardly there was dissension. As we listen in on the conversation of his sons around the campfire at night we note their jealousy. "Our father loves Joseph more than all the rest of us. Joseph may be the son of his old age, but as far as I am concerned he is nothing but an upstart. And can you believe our father's audacity in making him a 'varicolored tunic?'"[53]

It is no wonder that they hated him and could not speak to him on friendly terms.

---

52. Geikie, *The Holy Land and the Bible*, I:363.
53. I have based this imaginary discussion on 37:3-4 and other references such as.

This injudicious favoritism was the cause of smoldering resentment against their younger brother, and it erupted in ill-concealed hatred of Joseph when their father gave him the special tunic he had made.

The tunic Jacob gave Joseph has occasioned considerable debate. The King James Version translated *ketonet passim* a "coat of many colors." This is possible, though a better translation is a "robe with long sleeves" (cf. 2 Samuel 13:18-19). From 37:2c it is evident that Joseph, though only seventeen, was acting as an overseer[54] on his father's behalf.[55] Along with the special favors that Jacob was heaping on Joseph there was the belief on the part of Jacob's other sons that their father intended to confer on Joseph the right of primogeniture and leave the headship of the tribe to him.

---

54. Laborers wore tunics without sleeves so that nothing could hinder their movement. Supervisors wore garments with long sleeves to indicate their authority.
55. Cf. Bush, *Genesis*, II:220, who translates the latter part of verse 2 as "acting the shepherd over his brothers." He goes on to state, "However uncouth to our ears the phraseology, this is undoubtedly the exact rendering of the [original text]." And the occasion? Joseph, having been sent by his father to tend sheep with four of his brothers, namely, Dan, Naphtali, Gad, and Asher, brought to his father an evil report about them. This made them his enemies, whereas if the matter had been handled with discretion, Joseph might have had them as friends (since, as sons of Jacob's secondary wives, they always stood in the shadow of their brethren borne to either Leah or Rachel).

In the ancient Near East nothing was then, and still is, more common than that the firstborn succeed to this office. But there are notable exceptions. Examples of such exceptions are to be found in biblical as well as extra-biblical sources. For example, David selected Solomon, Bathsheba's son, to succeed him in preference to Adonijah or one of his brothers who were older than Solomon. In like manner Darius Hystaspis chose Xerxes, the firstborn of his beloved Atossa, in preference to his other sons who had been born before Xerxes.

Such elevation to prominence invariably caused trouble, and we are not surprised to read that Joseph's brothers "hated" him and could not speak kindly to him (37:4). Under such circumstances it is wise for one so honored to be careful and judicious in his conduct, avoid all forms of arrogance, and give others no occasion to act out their anger toward him. Joseph, perhaps because of his youth, did not exhibit such wisdom. Instead, he appears to have been impudent and confident of his father's protection. And Joseph might have succeeded had he not also had dreams implying his superiority over the members of his family. We read,

> Then Joseph had a dream, and when he told it to his brothers, they hated him even more. He said to them, "Please listen to this dream which I have had; for behold, we were binding sheaves in the field, and lo, my sheaf rose up and also stood erect; and behold, your sheaves gathered around and bowed down to my sheaf."

Then his brothers said to him, "Are you actually going to reign over us?" So they hated him even more for his dreams than for his words.

Now he had still another dream, and related it to his brothers, and said, "Lo, I have had still another dream; and behold, the sun and the moon and eleven stars were bowing down to me."

When he related it to his father, his father rebuked him and said to him, "What is this dream that you have had? Shall I and your mother[56] and your brothers actually come to bow ourselves down before you to the ground?"

His brothers were jealous of him, but his father kept the saying in mind (37:5-11).

The interpretation of these dreams leaves no doubt as to there meaning. In the first dream Joseph and his brothers were harvesting grain. His sheaf stood upright, and their sheaves came before his sheaf and paid special homage to his sheaf. Then, a short time later he had an even more grandiose dream. The sun and moon, representing Jacob and Leah, and eleven stars, representing his brothers, came and bowed down to him. This dream earned Joseph his father's rebuke, but Jacob (who had himself received divine communication via dreams), reflected deeply on what Joseph's dreams might reveal.

---

56. With Rachel's death, Leah had probably assumed the place of her dead sister.

In the course of time Jacob's sons extended their pastoral labors northward to Shechem.[57] When no word of their safety was received by the aging patriarch, he sent Joseph to check on their well-being (37:14). Joseph journeyed from the valley of Hebron to Shechem, but failed to find his brothers there. He was seen by a certain man, and when he asked Joseph what he was looking for, Joseph asked him if he had seen his brothers and their flock. The man fortuitously had heard them talking about going to Dothan,[58] and so directed Joseph northward toward the place of the "two wells" that lies on the East of the ancient road leading from Gilead across Esdraelon to the seacoast, and then south to Egypt.

According to visitors to the region, Joseph would have climbed the steep slope of the hill north of Samaria, and his descent easily would have been seen by his brothers (37:18). As he approached them, nine of them "plotted against him;" but Reuben was absent. Such was their hatred of Joseph that they did not hesitate to discuss his murder. But how were they to dispose of his body? The decision they reached was a simple one. They would throw his lifeless body into a pit, and then tell their father that a wild beast had eaten him.

---

57. C. R. Conder in *Tent Work in Palestine*, 2 vols. (London: Palestine Exploration Fund, 1880), I:107, provides a graphic description of the local flora and the fecundity of the region. See also Geikie, *The Holy Land and the Bible*, II:244; and Thomson, *The Land and the Book*, I:466.

58. *Macmillan Bible Atlas*, #46 (p. 44).

When Reuben learned of their plan, he opposed it, saying, "Let us not kill him. Do not shed his blood, but throw him into this pit" (37:20-22). Being the oldest, he apparently felt an obligation to protect his younger brother. Once the others had agreed not to kill Joseph, they stripped him of his long-sleeved coat and threw him into a pit[59] (little realizing that Reuben planned to rescue him at a later time). Then they sat down to enjoy the main meal of the day.[60] Something of their calloused indifference to Joseph's feelings is preserved for us in 42:21 where, years later, they recall Joseph's "distress of his soul" when he pleaded with them, but they would not listen.

While Jacob's sons were enjoying their meal they suddenly saw a caravan of Ishmaelites with their camels coming from Gilead, carrying spices and balm and myrrh to be sold in Egypt. It was not unusual for caravans to take this route, for the great highway from Gilead led past Dothan. The sight of this caravan, accompanied by Midianite merchants, put a new thought into the minds of Joseph's brothers. Instead of killing their younger brother or leaving him to die of starvation at the bottom of a pit, they could get rid of him without staining their hands with his blood by selling him, *and they could benefit from the sale* (37:26-27).

---

59. Often used as a well to catch water during the rainy season.
60. Bush, *Genesis*, II:232, writes that this meal involves something more than an ordinary meal. "In order to stifle the workings of conscience, they sat down to enjoy a joyous fest, eating, drinking, and making merry, regardless of the tears and anguish" of their victim in the pit.

Without delay Jacob's sons brought up Joseph from the well and sold him to the Ishmaelites for twenty pieces of silver (37:28).[61] They then killed a young goat and, after tearing Joseph's coat, they dipped it in the blood to give it the appearance of having been torn off Joseph when he was attacked by a wild animal.

Even if Jacob's sons concluded their stay at Dothan soon after they sold Joseph to the Ishmaelites, it still would have taken them several weeks to reach Hebron. Dr. William H. Thomson, who was intimately acquainted with the mores of those living in the Near East, wrote of their meeting with their father: "They surpassed themselves in heartlessness when they brought Joseph's torn, blood-stained coat to their father, and asked Jacob if he recognized it. It would be hard to conceive of a more detestable piece of hypocrisy than those mourning sons pretending that they knew nothing of what had happened to Joseph. But in the distant background is the picture of Jacob, practicing an imposition on his own father, only now to receive himself a tenfold heavier punishment"(37:32-33).[62]

The grief of Jacob was excessive. "Jacob tore his clothes, and put sackcloth on his loins and mourned for his son many days. And all his sons and all his daughters arose to comfort him, but he refused to be comforted, and said,

---

61. Josephus, *Antiquities of the Jews*, II:3:1-4. The price of a mature, strong slave was later set at thirty pieces of silver.

62. Thomson, *Life and Times of the Patriarchs*, 205-06.

'Surely I will go down to Sheol in mourning for my son.' So his father wept for him" (37:34-35). And being bereaved of Joseph, Jacob clung tenaciously to Benjamin, the only remaining child of his tenderly loved wife Rachel.

The chapter closes, however, with a hopeful postscript: "Meanwhile, the Midianites sold Joseph in Egypt to Potiphar, Pharaoh's officer, the captain of the bodyguard" (37:36). Like an enjoyable movie where the film makers hint at the possibility of a sequel, this verse indicates that we may assume that the story of Joseph is not over.

As we reflect on the crosscurrents that have been presented to us in this chapter, we note that it contrasts mankind's sin with God's grace. Perhaps the most important truth to penetrate our hearts as we consider the events of this story is the corrosive effects of envy (cf. Acts 7:9; and the counsel of David in Psalms 37:1 and 43:3). The difference between envy and covetousness is that we envy people and covet things. All that is recorded of Joseph's brothers–their anger, malice, conspiracy, cruelty, callous disregard for their brother's feelings, and deceit–sprang from envy (cf. Romans 1:29-30; Galatians 5:21, note the context of 5:19ff.).

Next we reflect upon the grace of God. After the psalmist had exhorted his readers not to fret because of evildoers, nor be envious of wrongdoers, he went on to encourage them to (1) trust in the Lord and do good; dwell in the land and cultivate faithfulness; (2) delight themselves in the Lord; (3) commit their way to the Lord; and, (4) confidently trust in Him (Psalm 37:1-6). In other words, by doing good they could nullify the malignancy of those who hated them.

In addition to this practical admonition, we also note in this chapter sin's eventual defeat. Sin may hinder God's plans, but it cannot nullify them. God's grace was evident in the experience of Joseph. When he was taken down to Egypt, he was purchased by an influential man named Potiphar. Then we read, *"And the Lord was with Joseph."* He became a successful man in the house of his master the Egyptian (cf. 39:1-3, emphasis added).

In much the same way the Lord is with us in all of the vicissitudes of life, and can prosper us if we commit our way to Him (Psalm 55:22; 1 Peter 5:6-7)!

CHAPTER 12

FAMINE RELIEF

Famines occupy a conspicuous place in Scripture, and are sometimes mentioned as one of the scourges that God sends to chastise men for their wickedness (cf. Leviticus 26:21, 26; Psalm 105:16; Lamentations 4:4-6; Ezekiel 14:21).

The Bible lists several causes of famine to explain why God's blessing was being withheld from His people (cf. Hosea 2:8-9; Haggai 1:6). These include (1) a plague of locusts;[63] or (2) the absence of the November/December rains[64] (1 Kings 17:1; Jeremiah 14:1-4; Amos 4:7-8). God's withdrawal of these early and latter rains resulted in the failure of crops to mature. In Egypt, on those rare occasions when the Nile did not rise, it resulted in the widespread deprivation of the staples upon which people depended for their survival (cf. 41:56-57).

The Journey to Egypt. Apparently the rains upon which Egypt depended did not come,[65] and in chapters 42–44 we read that Canaan also felt the famine impact. Because one of the trade routes linking Egypt with Syria ran through

---

63. *The National Geographic*, (1915), 511-50; *idem*, (1953), 545-62; *idem*, (1969), 202-27.
64. Bromiley, G. W., et al., eds. *The International Standard Bible Encyclopedia*, 4 vols. (Grand Rapids: Eerdmans, 1988), IV:35-36.

Hebron, it would have been natural for Jacob to hear that there was food in Egypt. Of course, the patriarch had no idea that food in Egypt was the result of Joseph's masterful planning.

> When Jacob heard that there was grain in Egypt, he said to his sons, "Why do you look at one another? I have heard that there is grain in Egypt; go down to that place and buy food for us there, that we may live and not die." So Joseph's ten brothers went down to buy grain in Egypt. But Jacob did not send Joseph's brother Benjamin with his brothers, for he said, "Lest some calamity befall him" (42:1-4).

Jacob's sons traveled to Egypt to buy food in company with others who were going there for the same purpose. However, before we consider what happened when Jacob's sons arrived in Egypt, we need to answer a pressing question: Why were the ten brothers listlessly standing about staring at one another and not taking the initiative to find food for their families?

---

65. The fruitfulness of Egypt depends upon the inundations of the Nile. These are occasioned by the tropical rains which fall upon the Abyssinian mountains. These rains depend upon climatic laws, yet there is scarcely a land on the earth in which famine has raged so often and so terribly as in Egypt. Cf. J. M'Clintock and J. Strong, *Encyclopedia of the Biblical, Theological, and Ecclesiastical Literature* (Grand Rapids: Baker, 2000), article on "Famine."

From references in the story to their feelings of guilt (cf. 42:21-22) it seems as if the thought of going to Egypt brought vividly to mind actions repressed for more than twenty years.[66] These memories had the effect of numbing their minds and stifling their emotions so that they became apathetic. It was only when their father commanded them that they made the journey, all the while trying to console themselves with the thought that Joseph was assuredly dead.

The route the brothers took has been described by the Oxford professor of history, George Rawlinson.[67] His description contains the unmistakable evidence of an eyewitness.

The Meeting with Joseph. Joseph, who was now Governor of Egypt, was 38 or 39 years old, and it had been more than 20 years since his brothers had sold him into slavery. On coming into his presence they bowed down before him with their faces to the earth--unknowingly fulfilling his early dream (37:5-8). Joseph, of course, recognized them. To determine if they had changed, Joseph treated them harshly, asked where they had come from, and accused them of being spies.

Joseph's brothers denied the charge, and gave as their explanation, "Your servants are twelve brothers in all, the sons of one man in the land of Canaan; and behold, the youngest is with our father today, and one is no longer

---

66. D. G. Benner, ed., *Baker Encyclopedia of Psychology* (Grand Rapids: Baker, 1985), 486-88.
67. Rawlinson, *Isaac and Jacob*, 147.

alive" (42:13). Joseph pretended that this explanation was insufficient and demanded that one of them return to Canaan and bring back their youngest brother to back up the truthfulness of their story. And with this summary judgment he put all ten of his brothers in prison (42:17).

At the end of three days they appeared before Joseph again, and he repeated his demand that one of them return to Canaan and bring to Egypt their younger brother. Speaking among themselves (for communication with Joseph was through an interpreter, 42:23) they said to one another, "Surely we are being punished because of our brother. We saw how distressed he was when he pleaded with us for his life, but we would not listen; that's why this distress has come upon us." And to this general discussion Reuben interposed his own account of what had happened, "Didn't I tell you not to sin against the boy? But you wouldn't listen! Now we must give an accounting for his blood" (42:21-22).

The impasse was resolved when Simeon was selected to remain behind as a hostage, and the brothers returned to their homes. The grain they had come to buy was placed in their sacks together with their money (42:25).[68]

Though Joseph appeared to treat them harshly, there is nothing more striking in his character than the utter absence of revengeful feelings."[69]

---

68. Geikie, *The Holy Land and the Bible*, I:239, describes the effect of the drought on the once-luxuriant land.
69. Thomas, *Genesis*, 407.

The Return to Canaan. The brothers had not gone far before they discovered the money in their sacks (42:26-38). Once again they were filled with fear, and they quickly associated this new circumstance with their past wrongdoing. On arriving home they told Jacob all that had happened to them. Their recounting of events was unvarnished, and there were no lies or deception of their father this time. Of course, they had to tell Jacob how the Governor had stated that there would be no future sale of grain to them unless Benjamin accompanied them, and to reinforce the seriousness of his demand, they had to tell Jacob that Simeon was being kept a hostage pending Benjamin's arrival.

Jacob's response was a pitiful display of self-centered commiseration: "You have bereaved me of my children: Joseph is no more, and Simeon is no more, and you would take Benjamin; all these things are against me." In this exhibition of "poor me" Jacob was reacting to his circumstances without giving thought to the possibility that the God, whom he professed to worship, might have a purpose in these events.

Jacob's reaction reinforces for us a belief in the providence of God. Outwardly, and from a human point-of-view, the prognosis seemed hopeless, but the Lord was working behind the scenes demonstrating that all things work together for good to those who love God, who are called according to His purpose.

Meanwhile, Joseph's reaction on seeing his brothers is one of genuine affection. It is true that he tested them to see if there had been any change in their attitude, but all that he said and did was prompted by love for them. Such is the power of forgiveness.

On the other hand, Jacob's sons illustrate for us the power of a guilty conscience. How often they had been reminded of their calloused disregard for the well-being of their younger brother is not told us, but to the best of their ability they had tried to repress all thought of what they had done. Decades later they were still tortured by their memories of their actions on that fateful day.

As chapter 42 closes we are given an illustration of the fallacy of assessing our circumstances based solely on outward appearances. Then, in spite of the fact that chapters 43–44 form a unit, we see how the Lord was orchestrating everything for the benefit of His people.

The Family's Desperate Need. Time passed, and it wasn't long before Jacob's large family again needed food.[70] This, of course, raised the issue of Benjamin and the Egyptian Governor's statement that they would not see his face again unless Benjamin accompanied his brothers.[71]

---

70. Jacob's family in Canaan exceeded sixty-six persons (46:26). When the wives of Jacob's sons were added to this number there would have been upwards of seventy-five mouths to feed.
71. Apart from Joseph's strong desire to see his younger brother, his demand that Benjamin come with the others may have been to assure himself that Benjamin was still alive and had not suffered a fate similar to his own.

At first, when Jacob's sons insisted that Benjamin accompany them to Egypt, Jacob resorted to blame: "Why did you deal so wrongfully with me as to tell the man whether you had still another brother?" Joseph, of course, had specifically asked about their family, and his enquiry had elicited their response. Because the need of Jacob's large family was urgent, Judah agreed to become surety for Benjamin and, somewhat reassured Jacob commended them all to the grace of God and the protection of *El Shaddai,* "God Almighty." This done, he again descended into fatalistic self-pity, saying, "If I am bereaved of my children, I am bereaved!" (43:6, 14*b*).

The Governor's Glad Reception. As Jacob's sons returned they had no idea what awaited them. As a precaution they took extra money in their sacks, and with Benjamin accompanying them, they went to Egypt (43:15-34). On seeing Benjamin Joseph decided to entertain his brothers in his own home. This caused them to experience acute anxiety, and they concluded that they needed to admit what had happened. Speaking to Joseph's steward, they said:

> "O my lord, we indeed came down the first time to buy food; but it happened, when we came to the encampment, that we opened our sacks, and there, each man's money was in the mouth of his sack, our money in full weight; so we have brought it back in our hand. And we have brought down other money in our hands to buy food. We do not know who put our money in our sacks" (43:20-22).

The steward replied, "Peace be with you, do not be afraid. Your God and the God of your father has given you treasure in your sacks; I had your money." Then he brought Simeon out to them (43:23).

When Joseph arrived at his home for the noon meal, his brothers again prostrated themselves before him. Then they gave him the present they had brought from Canaan (42:11). However, the sight of Benjamin, "his mother's son," was too much for Joseph, and he hurried out of the room and into his bedroom in order to weep there. Then he washed his face (43:30-31), and returned to join them for dinner.

Joseph personally seated his brothers by themselves, the "firstborn according to his birthright and the youngest according to his youth" (43:33). The Egyptians, of course, ate by themselves, and he ate alone. All of this had a profound effect on Joseph's brothers. Joseph also took food and drink to them from his own table, but gave Benjamin five times as much as any of his brothers. This gave him the opportunity to discover the feelings of his brothers towards Benjamin: Were they envious of him or were they resentful of the favor being shown him?

An Unexpected Turn of Events. The next day Joseph's brothers set out on their return journey. They did not know that Joseph had instructed his steward to fill their sacks with as much wheat as they would hold, and they were unaware of the fact that Joseph's special goblet had been placed in Benjamin's sack (44:2, 5).

This, of course, raises the question, Did Joseph use divination? The answer is most assuredly, No. It is possible that when trying to determine the truth or falsity of a matter, Joseph may have called for his special goblet, commanded that water be poured into it, and pretend to discern who was guilty and who was not by looking into the goblet. Among a superstitious people such acts would have a profound effect, and if the guilty party did not confess his crime, his facial expression would most assuredly betray him.

When the goblet was found in Benjamin's sack the brothers were horrified. Instead of allowing Benjamin to return to face Joseph alone, they all returned to Egypt.

Joseph was still in the house when Judah and his brothers came in, and they threw themselves to the ground before him. Joseph said to them, "What is this you have done? Don't you know that a man like me can find things out by divination?"

Judah, realizing that to argue their innocense before the Governor might antagonism him, said, "What can we say to my lord? What can we say? How can we prove our innocence? God has uncovered your servants' guilt. We are now my lord's slaves--we ourselves and the one who was found to have the cup" (44:14-16).

If Judah believed that Benjamin had indeed stolen Joseph's goblet, then his use of "we" and "our" is most revealing, and instead of abandoning Benjamin to whatever fate might lie in store for him he stated the willingness of all the brothers to be punished along with Benjamin.

Joseph, however, would not allow Judah's proposal to stand. The one in whose sack the goblet was found should bear his punishment, and the rest could go to their father.

It would seem as if Joseph's strategy was to test his brothers to see if they would be prepared to sacrifice Benjamin for their own safety. It also may be that he wanted to be alone with Benjamin, at least for a time, so that he could satisfy his own intense longing for fellowship with his mother's younger son.[72]

With Joseph's brothers before him, and sensing that they had changed over the years, he commanded all his servants to leave the room. Then turning to his brothers, he said, "*I am Joseph.*" At first the shock of this revelation was too much for them. After a tearful reunion, Joseph sent his brothers back to his father with news that he was still alive, and that they should all come to Egypt where he would look after them for the remainder of the famine.

Jacob did so, and enjoyed the closeness of his son for seventeen years before he died.

As we consider the many lessons that lie latent in these chapters, we take note of God's patient discipline of His people. Though the sin of selling Joseph into slavery had

---

72. But there is another possible explanation. The way in which Judah refers to God having found out their iniquity may allude to their actions decades earlier when they sold Joseph into slavery. Now, with a twist of poetic justice, he expresses his, and their, willingness to likewise become slaves in Egypt.

been repressed by his brothers, and at times was almost forgotten, yet the Lord kept using different circumstances as a means of bringing them to repentance. They were unaware of the fact that the seemingly ordinary events of their life were in reality being the means of a most thorough examination of their character. And so it is with us. As we walk with the Lord we realize that nothing is trivial.

We also observe how dangerous it is to misinterpret events and conclude that everything is against us. We also tend to mistake punishment for chastisement. In Jacob's case, however, the Lord was using outward circumstances, as painful as they might be, to refine Jacob's character and make him into a "prince with God."

And finally, we need the constant reminder that there is something of Jacob in all of us. There are times when we walk with the Lord, but in between these high points there are valleys when we are led by our fleshly impulses. The Christian life is one of discipline, and if we are going to become men and women of mature faith, we need to daily live in obedience to His Word.

www.ingramcontent.com/pod-product-compliance
Lightning Source LLC
Chambersburg PA
CBHW070927160426
43193CB00011B/1600